IF THEY WON'T BEND, BREAK THEM!®

Tips, Tactics and Strategies You Need to Negotiate Like a Pro

GEOFFREY MICHAEL

CANNON
COMMUNICATIONS™

Cannon Communications

CANNON
COMMUNICATIONS™

LCCN: 2024902280
ISBN: 979-8-9910320-0-1

Table of Contents

Dedication

This book is dedicated to my father, George Michael, the first auctioneer from the New England states inducted into the National Auctioneers Hall of Fame in Overland Park, Kansas. His induction was a significant achievement because 57 auctioneers from around the country preceded him during the prior 25 years. He also cofounded the New Hampshire Auctioneers Association and was its first president.

As a boy, I worked at his estate liquidations, antique sales, and household goods auctions conducted in his artfully appointed and aptly named "auction barn" on the old Milton road. With its wooden bleacher seats, sand floor, and giant wood stoves, the barn attracted an eclectic assortment of country folk who showed up weekly to be entertained and hopefully steal a few bargains. If we couldn't sell something and it would burn, it went straight into the wood stoves to heat the barn. Even if it wouldn't burn, those stoves ran so hot they'd incinerate almost anything we wanted to get rid of.

I learned the ropes about wheeling and dealing as a runner at his auctions. I got a real education at an early age about how to persuade and influence people who understood the value of a dollar and refused to spend one more than they had to. It was all cash in those days, including silver certificates and coins containing actual silver. There was no plastic money, so they could only spend what they had in their pockets, and that's where the bidding had to stop.

Over several years working those auctions, I dealt with many street-smart, old-school Yankees and cultivated business instincts that you can't acquire in traditional institutions of higher learning. Perhaps most importantly, I developed an ability to read people and predict how they would react under dynamic circumstances without relying on what they said and did. As I explain in this book, that skill is my most important asset when facing off against the best negotiators in the world.

———————————

Thanks to one of my brothers for inspiring the title of this book. While he engaged in protracted negotiations over a financial dispute with a contractor who had completed repairs to his house, I offered advice on settling their disagreement. After considerable discussions, the contractor wouldn't budge from his original position. My brother reported that despite his best efforts to resolve their differences, "they wouldn't bend" to any of his demands. My immediate reaction was, "If they won't bend, break them!" which became a registered trademark.

The significance of my reaction will become crystal clear as you read this book. Until I reach a point where the other party refuses to budge no matter what, then the real negotiating has yet to begin. Please read that last sentence again. If you settle with someone who can't or won't move their position in your favor, you're leaving money on the table that belongs in your pocket. My primary mission is to provide you with the tools and confidence needed to make that happen. Please stick with me and see for yourself. If you do, I guarantee you'll recover the cost of this book hundreds of times over.

About the Author

This book contains my opinions, observations, and recommendations but is not about me. It's not a memoir, life story, or anything close to that. I'm smart enough to realize no one would buy it if I wrote such a book. I assure you that virtually every word will help you become a successful negotiator, apart from some random facts about me summarized over the following several pages.

Why include any information about me when I know you're looking for advice about negotiating? It's a fair question, and here's my answer. You've probably never heard of me, have no idea who I am, and will never cross paths with me again after you read this book. If I'm considering whether or not to follow the advice of someone I don't know, I'd like more to go on than blind faith. At a minimum, I want to know something about their background, experience, education, interests, and what makes them tick. Anything they can provide to bolster my confidence in what they tell me is worth my time and attention.

Call it curiosity emanating from an inquiring mind. An overview of my background provides some perspective on the experiences that formed the foundation for my career, greatly influenced my thinking, and helped prepare me for what was to come in my adult life. I acquired most of my knowledge about negotiation through on-the-job training and trial and error. I never studied the subject in school or approached it from an academic or theoretical perspective. It's all based on the real-world application of my cumulative life experience, both personal and professional.

I'm an alumnus of the United States Air Force Academy (USAFA) in Colorado Springs, Colorado. After graduating with a bachelor of science degree and commission as a second lieutenant, I served six years on active duty in the project management field as an Air Force procurement officer. I developed and managed advanced aviation systems and space communications programs.

I have a strong background in personal finance, investing, economics, stock markets, marketing, and aviation. I've written articles on selected subjects published in the *Wall Street Journal*, *Forbes*, and *Entrepreneur*. I'm a member in good standing of the State Bars of California and New Hampshire and the Bar of the U.S. Supreme Court. I've also completed the N.H. Superior Court Rule 170 Civil Mediation Training.

My primary reason for attending USAFA was to become an astronaut. My fascination with space goes way back to my childhood when space exploration was in its infancy. I clearly remember the night my father awakened my two older brothers and me and drove us to the local radio station located at the top of a hill. He knew the people who operated the station, and we were there in the early morning hours of 05 October 1957 to witness an extraordinary event.

The hill's elevation provided an excellent vantage point to view the night sky without the interference of city lights. It was a dark, cloudless night with ideal weather conditions. Inside the station, we could hear the constant beep of the Sputnik 1 satellite as its orbit approached our position. The chief engineer had been monitoring its path all night and had data from the National Advisory Committee for Aeronautics (predecessor to the National Aeronautics and Space Administration—NASA) indicating that it would pass almost directly overhead.

To my astonishment, we could see a spec of light gliding across the night sky. It was barely visible, no bigger than a distant star, but the reflected light was just enough to illuminate what I thought was the tiny spacecraft. On the fiftieth anniversary of Sputnik's launch, I discovered that what I saw circling overhead was probably the second stage of the booster rocket in a nearly identical orbit to the spacecraft.

Although I knew nothing about the principles of orbital mechanics and astronautics, the space bug had bitten me in a way I didn't comprehend at such an early age. When Star Trek hit the airwaves in 1966, I was an immediate fan and have remained one ever since.

The closest I ever came to space was a training flight aboard the modified C-135A "Vomit Comet" at Wright-Patterson Air Force Base. With its seats removed and the cabin interior fully padded, this aircraft was the primary weightless trainer for NASA astronauts. It was a thrilling experience, and I still have the certificate documenting my flight.

My USAFA classmates from 37th Squadron assemble annually for a reunion at an away football game. We won't settle for one-day reunions. Ours usually last four days, long enough to where we don't want to leave on the final day. We survived tough times together during our first year at the academy, creating a lasting, unbreakable bond. Our entire class holds a reunion in Colorado Springs every five years.

C-Springs was one of three finalists for the academy's permanent location. The site selection committee had some concerns regarding the Colorado site and its turbulent weather, given its location on the eastern slope of the Rocky Mountains. It was known for its thin air, high winds, and snowy winters and was often not conducive to safe flying for beginner pilots.

One prominent committee member was Brigadier General Charles Lindbergh, U.S. Air Force Reserve. He planned to fly over the area surrounding the proposed site, paying particular attention to possible wind shear off the mountains. His mission was to assess flying safety issues and report his findings to the committee.

What follows is a recounting of what transpired after three committee members, including Lindbergh, arrived in C-Springs. The text is quoted directly from the *Air Force Academy Heritage—The Early Years*, by George V. Fagan, Brigadier General, USAF (Ret.).

After arriving at Peterson Field, [Dr. Virgil M. Hancher, president of the State University of Iowa], [Mr. Merrill C. Meigs, vice president of the Hearst Corporation], and Lindbergh got into a staff car and rode off to inspect the terrain of the so-called Pike View site. They paid particular attention to the areas designated for the proposed runways. All agreed that an aerial survey would prove most helpful. They then drove to the nearby Pine Valley Airport, where a small flying school was being operated. Lindbergh wanted to rent a Stinson 90 and take Meigs and Hancher along as passengers.

Since Lindbergh was wearing civilian clothes, the old-time, hard-boiled pilot who was the manager of the airport did not recognize him. Meigs gleefully described the scene:

"Do you know how to fly?" asked the airport manager.

"I think I can fly," Lindbergh answered quietly.

"Do you have a license?" was the next query.

"Yes, I have a license," said Lindbergh.

"Well," said the manager, "I'll have to see your license. If you will come into my office, I'll look over your papers."

We walked into the little office with its broken-down furniture and cracked walls. The manager seated himself importantly at a desk, got out some papers, and said to Lindbergh, "Let's see your license."

Lindbergh, of course, has about a dozen licenses from all over the world. Each bears his photograph. When he laid them out on the desk, the airport manager's neck began to redden. The color mounted to his face as he stared incredulously at Lindbergh, then back at the licenses.

"You ain't Charles Lindbergh, be you?" he stammered.

"Yes, I am," said Lindbergh.

"My God!" exclaimed the manager and almost collapsed on the desk in embarrassment.

After his flight over the Colorado Springs site, General Lindbergh concluded that the area was suitable for flying training. This positive pronouncement by one of the world's most famous aviators put to rest the many objections that had been raised both in and out of the Air Force about the Colorado Springs site.

General Lindbergh possessed all the leverage he needed in that discussion to secure his flight to conduct the survey. As you'll soon discover, leverage is everything in my negotiating world. When you have it, you use it. When you don't, you do whatever it takes to get it or work around it.

I'm proud to say I've made four successful takeoffs in a Fairchild C-119 Flying Boxcar aircraft without risking my life by landing in one. I did this while completing the U.S. Army Basic Airborne Course at Fort Benning, Georgia, as part of my cadet training. The C-119 came into service in 1947 as a post-World War II cargo transport aircraft. It saw extensive service during the Korean War to transport troops and equipment.

I wrote an article about my airborne experiences for Checkpoints Magazine, published by the USAFA Association of Graduates. My description of the takeoff explains why I wasn't disappointed that I never landed in this aircraft. Jump Week is the last of three weeks of training, and here's an excerpt from the article that describes what the preparation and takeoff for the first jump were like.

Finally, Jump Week arrived, and I was glad all the ground training was behind us. Like every other summer day in Georgia, our first day was hot and steamy. The Fairchild C-119 Flying Boxcars were parked on the ramp at Eubanks Field, ready to lift us skyward into the wild blue yonder. We climbed aboard with all our gear strapped on. Emotions were high, and there was a feeling of excitement and anticipation in the air. The past two weeks had been physically challenging, but it was now a mental challenge more than anything else.

I was sweating profusely, not from fear, but from the heat, humidity, and the weight of the parachute on my back. It only worsened as we jammed together in the troop seats in a plane with virtually no air circulation or ventilation. The flight crew cranked up the engines and edged our aircraft in line for takeoff. I first thought they should have nicknamed this the Rattletrap instead of the Boxcar. Every rivet, joint, and moving part creaked, groaned, squeaked, clanged, and moaned as we taxied into position. When we got the green light for takeoff and they revved up the engines, I thought I must have fallen into an eggbeater. The aircraft shook, bounced, and vibrated down the runway until we rotated and ascended into the hazy sky above.

Once aloft, the rattling was slightly more subdued, but hearing the jumpmaster's commands in the cargo bay was still difficult. I wondered if this wasn't part of the Army's master plan. After all, here I was in this old, slow, rattletrap of an airplane, sweating like a river through my fatigues, my ears ringing like a church bell from all the noise, and stuffed into what amounted to a flying sardine can. The quickest way to end this misery was to jump out and end it, and it was a far better option than risking a landing in that crate. The sooner I got out that door, the better. If the Army had a strategy to motivate us to jump, it was working to perfection. I couldn't wait.

We made four jumps from the C-119 and were looking forward to our final jump from a Lockheed C-141 Starlifter cargo jet. Five jumps qualify you for the basic parachutist badge. The Starlifter was a lot more comfortable for the jumpers and certainly lacked the same motivating force to thrust yourself out the door. The entire experience was a tremendous thrill, and the Army Airborne team that conducted our training was exceptional. It became crystal clear very quickly why our paratroopers are the best in the world.

During the summer of my second year at the academy, my entire class received survival, evasion, resistance, and escape training (SERE). This training subjected many of us to extensive water-boarding, otherwise portrayed in some media as "enhanced inter-rogation." It's always amazed me how many Americans consider the waterboarding of terrorists as torture, but not when imposed on our military forces. For some of them, it's simply part of their required training. I can definitively say that SERE hardened me up for the challenges I would face after graduation. Did it help me become a better negotiator? Absolutely.

My brothers and I have had a sixties rock 'n' roll band since our teens. My role has always been rhythm guitar, and I also sing lead and backup vocals. We've never figured out how to make money doing this, so we've always done it for fun. It makes our lives easier because the Internal Revenue Service knows nothing about it. My go-to instrument is a 1980s-era Fender Stratocaster, but I have a few other guitars kicking around that get far less use.

The oldest is a right-handed Höfner 500/1 electric "violin bass," virtually identical to Paul McCartney's left-handed version. He didn't own a bass before 1961 because, up until that point, he had primarily played the piano. Stuart Sutcliffe played bass, and Pete Best was still the drummer. When Sutcliffe announced he'd be leaving the band to return to school to study fine art, McCartney visited the Steinway Musikhaus in Hamburg, Germany, where the band had taken a residency.

The Beatles were relatively unknown then, and the final lineup didn't yet exist. Nevertheless, Höfner apparently manufactured a custom left-handed model specifically for him. There are no records or evidence that Höfner ever produced a left-handed 500/1 before McCartney ordered his. That has to be one of the best marketing decisions ever made because it put the company firmly on the map. The British Invasion and the sixties rock era featured many other musicians using the same bass and a variety of Höfner instruments. There are thousands of worldwide photographs and videos of McCartney holding that bass.

I bought my bass in a private sale from a young man who had received it as a gift from his grandmother. When she asked him what he'd like for Christmas one year, he told her he'd like a new guitar and amplifier. She visited the nearest music store and loved the look of the Höfner. The salesman recommended a Vox amp to go along with it.

When he received the generous gifts on Christmas Day, he thanked his grandmother without mentioning that he had no idea how to play the bass. He was taking lessons on the six-string guitar. Unfortunately, she didn't know the difference when she went shopping. He lacked the heart to ask her to return them, so he put them up for sale as a package deal. In addition to the Höfner, he was selling a Vox Super Beatle AC-100 amplifier with two Celestion T-100 15" speakers, complete with frame and casters. The total asking price was $300. Although technically used gear, the bass and amp were in brand-new condition. He planned to use the proceeds to buy the equipment he wanted, hoping his grandmother would overlook the difference months later.

I didn't need the amp because I'd recently purchased a blonde Fender Bassman, so I offered him $150 for the bass alone. He accepted the offer. The bass has increased exponentially in value since then, but I've kicked myself ever since for not buying the Super Beatle, too. Those amps are extremely rare and difficult to find in good condition. Any quality, high-profile gear from that era would have been an excellent investment. Who knew?

I also have a Martin D12-35 12-string acoustic, but my real prize is a six-string acoustic custom-made by José Luis Díaz Reyes in Paracho de Verduzco, Michoacán, Mexico. It all started many years ago when I read a magazine article about the town of Paracho, whose artisans are premier makers of guitars and vihuelas. Known throughout Mexico and much of the world, an estimated 90% of the town's population of 38,000 is involved in the production of stringed instruments. While most manufacturing occurs in factories, small shops line the streets where the masters craft their instruments entirely by hand. Some will let you observe as they work on guitars, mandolins, concheras, vihuelas, and acoustic bass guitars. When Spanish missionaries discovered how skilled the indigenous people were at woodworking, they taught them the techniques needed to produce the instruments.

The only artisan mentioned by name in the article was Mr. Reyes, who had won the annual competition for producing the best guitar in its category. Known as the Feria Nacional de la Guitarra, it's a weeklong event that attracts guitar enthusiasts from around the world. Mr. Reyes started as a young boy by helping his grandfather make violins. He selected the woods to be used and quickly discovered he had natural woodworking skills. By the time he was 13, he was making guitars from scratch and selling them in his grandfather's shop. I cut the article from the magazine and filed it away, thinking I'd someday make it to Mexico and purchase a handmade guitar from him.

About two decades later, while reviewing my files, I discovered the article about Paracho. I hadn't made it there, and I was concerned that my window of opportunity might be closing. While I didn't know Mr. Reyes's age, I could tell from the article that he was one of the elder master craftsmen, and I couldn't count on him working forever. I wrote a letter in English and addressed it to José Luis Díaz Reyes, Paracho, Mexico. I explained that I wanted him to make me a custom guitar and included some general design details and the types of wood to use. I mailed the letter and hoped it would somehow find its way to him.

Three months passed without a reply, and I assumed my letter never arrived. Then, I received a postcard from Julie at the Frog's Leap Winery in Napa Valley, California. She explained that she'd just returned from a trip to Mexico, including a stop in Paracho and a visit to Mr. Reyes's shop. When he recognized she was American, he pulled out my letter and showed it to her. Fortunately, she spoke Spanish and was able to translate it for him. He told her he'd been holding my letter for months, and she was the first person to visit his shop who could translate English into Spanish. Her note to me said he was looking forward to making me a guitar and to please send him more details written in Spanish. She also provided me with the complete mailing address for his shop, 361 Calle 20 de Noviembre.

I communicated with him via regular mail since email didn't yet exist. Luckily, a member of my program office staff spoke fluent Spanish. He translated all correspondence in both directions. Throughout the next few months, Mr. Reyes and I exchanged letters that nailed down the exact specifications for the guitar. We agreed that I would pay him half the price at the start and the remaining half following delivery to my home in the United States. Our deal depended on mutual trust, and I was confident he'd live up to his end of the bargain.

His final letter informed me of the expected delivery date via Mexicana Airlines air freight. Shortly after that, I received notice from U.S. Customs that a crate for me had arrived and provided instructions for pickup. I showed up all decked out in my best suit, thinking this might positively influence the people I was about to deal with. This shipment was the first time I'd ever received anything that had to pass through Customs, and I didn't know what to expect.

They wheeled out the crate, and apparently, no one had opened it. I was happy to see that because the contents could be easily damaged if not opened carefully. They only asked, "What's in the crate?" Of course, they already knew the answer based on the shipping documents, but they wanted to hear it from me. I knew they didn't have to believe me or the records, so I related the sequence of events that preceded the guitar production, starting with the magazine article that led me to Mr. Reyes. They found the story fascinating but, more importantly, believable. I then offered proof and pulled out the article, the postcard sent from the Frog's Leap Winery, and all the letters from Mr. Reyes with the stamped envelopes. That nailed it.

Any suspicions they had of a drug shipment or other contraband vanished. They turned the crate over to me without opening it, and I was on my way. When I got home, I found out just how lucky I was. I carefully dismantled the crate without knowing how securely the guitar was packed. I also vacuumed as I went along to avoid dust settling inside the guitar. The process took me about an hour but was necessary and worthwhile. The guitar emerged in pristine condition. Mr. Reyes had told me that several of the luthiers in town had tested it at his request and told him it was one of the finest guitars he'd ever produced. Once I played it for the first time, I had no reason to doubt him.

My father regularly picked up a truckload of merchandise from Sears, Roebuck and Co. to supplement the consignments he sold at his auctions. He provided a reliable mechanism for Sears to sell new items that had been discontinued, returned, or had missing parts, minor scratches, or damage. One of his loads had a new Silvertone tenor saxophone that was given to me because I was taking lessons on the clarinet. Musicians know the transition was easy because they're both keyed in Bb. At the time, Sears contracted with several manufacturers, including Conn, Martin, and Buescher, to make their instruments. I set the sax aside when I failed to perfect a technique allowing me to sing and play simultaneously.

Many years ago, I drove cross-country in a 27-year-old car. If you think only a fool would do that, you're right, especially considering it was a 1979 Mazda RX-7. I knew full well that in the event of a breakdown on I-70 in the middle of Kansas, it wouldn't be easy to find replacement parts for a rotary engine. Anyone who's ever driven that road knows you can travel for miles and miles without seeing one exit sign. Then, when you do see an exit, it's connected to a dirt road that seems to disappear into nowhere. Before I left Los Angeles, my mechanic assured me the car would make it with no problem. It turns out he was exactly right. Good mechanics can be hard to find, and Steve is one of the best. Thanks, Steve!

I've conducted live negotiation seminars for over fifteen years that provide tips and information for developing negotiating strategies to help attendees personally and professionally. Understanding negotiating principles is invaluable to anyone involved in management, business, finance, and procurement, even if negotiating isn't their primary role in the company. Seminar attendees leave with vital knowledge of the bedrock principles and skills necessary to negotiate effectively for the company and themselves. These seminars evolved and expanded over the years and provided the foundation for the contents of this book.

Introduction

This is the best book about negotiation ever written. If I didn't believe that, I wouldn't ask you to spend your time reading it.

Given the number of available books about negotiation, my claim that this one is the best of them undoubtedly sounds audacious, egotistical, and braggadocious. In my experience, it's the confidence level necessary to succeed as a top negotiator. I can draw a bright line between confidence and arrogance. Leave your arrogance at the door, but bring every ounce of confidence and preparation you possess to the negotiating table. If I'm on the other side of that table and I sense your confidence is lacking, I will crush you in negotiations (figuratively speaking).

Writing this book wasn't my idea. In April 2014, I was an enrichment lecturer aboard the Silversea Silver Spirit during its Atlantic crossing from Ft. Lauderdale to Barcelona. I split my negotiation seminar into four one-hour sessions spread throughout the two-week voyage. Video recordings of these presentations were available so passengers who couldn't attend in person would have the opportunity to view them in their suites at their convenience.

Later in the evening, after the first presentation, a passenger who said he'd enjoyed the video playback approached me in the Panorama Lounge. He asked me if I had written a book about negotiation, and I said it had never occurred to me. When he asked why, I told him several books were currently available, and I didn't know if there was a compelling need for another one.

He then asked if I could recommend one of those books for him to read. I replied that I'd never read a book on the topic because I learned everything I knew by actually doing it. I wasn't aware of any book that could measure up to that hard reality. I acquired my knowledge and experience by conducting actual negotiations, learning the ropes through trial and error, and graduating from the school of hard knocks. There's nothing like duking it out in the real world to sharpen your skills swiftly. Although I knew a handful of popular books, I wouldn't recommend one I hadn't read myself.

Not long after that encounter, I conducted a negotiation seminar for a group of insurance company executives in Aventura, Florida. After it concluded, one of the attendees asked me if I had published a book about negotiation or if I could recommend a good one. I replied "no" to both questions and gave him the same explanation I'd provided to the cruise passenger. He was somewhat surprised that I couldn't recommend one but even more surprised when I admitted I'd never read a book about negotiation.

This pattern repeated itself at subsequent seminars. People kept asking me what negotiation books I'd read and which ones I'd recommend. My response was always the same, but I began to feel embarrassed that I'd never read one book on a subject about which I claimed specific expertise. I had to do something about that, and I did. I read four popular bestselling books on the topic over several months. I'm sorry to report that, with few exceptions, it was mostly a waste of time.

While the flaws are too numerous to explain in detail, I'll summarize by saying the books need more focus on practical advice that most people seek for real-life negotiations. That's when I decided to write my book, with two overarching promises I vowed to keep.

First, I would refrain from negotiation theories dreamed up by college professors and career academics who spend more time hanging out in the faculty lounge than in actual negotiations. Anyone can profess untested theories and abstract concepts that may or may not work. Trust me, many of them don't.

Experience as a corporate executive or Ivy League college professor doesn't automatically qualify you to write a book about negotiation. I understand the game of football, but I'd never consider authoring a book about it. I'll leave that to someone like Tom Brady. Studying football theory and playing the game are two completely different things. Professional football represents the ultimate version of the school of hard knocks taken to the extreme.

When I read those four books, I hoped to pick up valuable pointers for my seminars. That didn't happen. There's no substitute for diving into the trenches of a complex negotiation where hundreds of millions of dollars are on the line. You quickly discover that all those theories sound impressive in the pages of a book but throw you against a wall when confronted by an adversary who doesn't subscribe to any theories whatsoever. Their goal is to beat you by whatever means necessary. Damn the theories; full speed ahead!

Second, I wanted my book to be a handy guide that everyone can use, whether you're negotiating to buy a used boat or a Fortune 500 company. I cite straightforward examples from my life illustrating fundamental principles that apply across the board for any negotiating scenario.

A strong desire to share my knowledge and experience with fellow USAFA graduates and current cadets greatly influenced my writing this book. They were a silent, motivating force behind the chapter titled "Great Leaders Negotiate." I believe it's vitally important for military officers to understand the commonality of skills needed to lead and negotiate effectively.

I'd enjoy the opportunity to personally interact with the cadets on the subject of negotiation at the annual Air Force Academy National Character and Leadership Symposium (NCLS). It's a flagship event featuring presentations from a diverse cross section of military, corporate, academic, and athletic contributors. Until that opportunity presents itself, this book is the best way to reach as many cadets as possible.

This perfect storm of incentives all pointed in one direction, and I considered engaging a larger audience beyond those attending my in-person seminars. The answer was this book.

My approach to writing it had nothing to do with untested theories, assumptions, or any other imagined tricks to make you a successful negotiator. I provide general rules and personally tested fundamental principles I've used in practically every negotiation I've ever done. They were all learned the hard way through real-life, real-time, on-the-job training.

I can't guarantee my approach will work for you because we all come from different backgrounds, have distinct personalities, and possess diverse skill sets. Since our ability to negotiate effectively depends on many factors I discuss in this book, the best I can do is explain how to integrate whatever skills you have into becoming the most effective negotiator possible.

Negotiation is an art, not a science, so there are no right or wrong answers, only better answers. The positive takeaway of that reality is that you can contribute unique skills and abilities that no one else has and learn from others with more experience than you. I've participated in enough negotiations to expect each one will reveal something new that I've never seen or experienced before. That's the kind of challenge I like and have benefitted from over the years.

Everything is negotiable, no matter how large or small the cost. A top-notch negotiation strategy can save you and your business huge sums of money. We all conduct dozens of negotiations daily in our personal and professional lives. Most of the time, we don't realize they're taking place. I'll provide you with vital knowledge of the bedrock principles and confidence necessary to negotiate effectively regardless of the circumstances.

Most negotiations involve some form of confrontation. The word "confrontation" has a negative connotation, but it doesn't have to be an unpleasant experience in the context of a negotiation.

Any face-to-face encounter is technically a confrontation, but most are decidedly friendly. I go into every negotiation knowing there will be conflicting ideas and opinions, but my overarching goal is maintaining a noncombative posture.

That's not to say things can't get heated and contentious at times, especially when large sums of money are involved and getting an expedited deal is crucial. If you're not the type who can cope with the stress and pressures of high-stakes encounters, you should avoid career choices that will regularly subject you to such negotiations. You're likely to encounter rude, overbearing, and sometimes frightening people who will attempt to pressure you into submitting to their demands. Succeeding in that environment requires an iron gut, homework, street smarts, and unblinking discipline. These keys will unlock your ability to get the best deal possible under very trying circumstances.

Sometimes, getting angry is an effective technique, but gratuitous anger meted systematically throughout a negotiation will quickly be ignored and likely backfire. Use anger as an action, but avoid it as a reaction. Go ahead and get angry to make your point, but not in retaliation for what the other party said or did. However, I do it sparingly at the risk of squandering its intended effect and ultimately working against me.

Negotiating is a part of everyday life, but it's critical to your success in business. A poor negotiation can seriously wound a company just as quickly as losing key customers. While most negotiating strategies seem like common sense, it's relatively easy for people to get caught up in the moment's emotions and ignore their basic instincts. Emotion, luck, and magic have no place in a successful negotiation.

While experienced negotiators sometimes refer to their methods as the "negotiating game," it's a misnomer for a process where the stakes are often remarkably high. When it's your money on the line, you must always check your ego at the door and keep your eye on the big picture. It's a game you want to win because you succeeded in influencing and persuading others to have your way.

One hint I'll pass on before showtime is to be on the lookout for sandbagging. It's a form of trickery that originated in the 1800s, apparently based on sneaking up behind a person and hitting them with a sandbag. It became a symbol of doing something to an unsuspecting person by surprise when they had no way of knowing what was coming or defending themselves. The action evolved to a point where a physical act was no longer required. Sandbagging also describes storytelling designed to fool people into believing something the storyteller knows to be substantively misleading or an intentional exaggeration.

In the business world, it's taken on a different meaning with a similar connotation. In a nutshell, the term depicts the art of promising less while delivering more. Usually, overdelivering is a good thing and should be encouraged. Isn't that a better outcome than making promises you fail to keep?

It depends on your perspective and which side of the seesaw you're sitting on. If you're a stockholder in a publicly-held corporation, you know the management routinely provides sales and earnings forecasts to gauge the progress and profitability of the company. Such information is regularly used for analytical purposes, including current and forward-looking metrics such as price-to-earnings (P/E) ratios. Setting expectations is a significant driver for Wall Street firms that buy and sell stocks based on several financial metrics. Consistently beating expectations often leads to higher stock prices, while the inverse is also true. So, the game that's played is to dependably exceed lowered expectations.

The same trickery can be used in negotiations when one side intentionally understates its bargaining position to fool the opposing party into assuming they have the upper hand. If someone is sandbagging you, the danger is you'll fall for it and become overconfident in your ability to execute your negotiation strategy.

Consequently, you're more prone to letting your guard down and opening yourself up to tactics that might not otherwise work.

It's a frequently used psychological weapon that succeeds if you succumb to the deception and fail to maintain vigilance. It's imperative to research, understand, and anticipate who you're dealing with. If the other side undersells its strengths and expertise and oversells its weaknesses and inabilities, you're the victim of sandbagging. They might even paint a picture of a degenerating financial condition intended to convey a message they have no room to negotiate.

The tactics and strategies used in various negotiations may change, but the basic principles remain the same. This book will provide you with the toolkit you can use anytime and anywhere to be successful. I assure you it's unlike any book about negotiation you've ever seen or read.

Since the two biggest purchases made by most people are their home and car, I wrote separate chapters focusing on those two asset classes. However, many tips and techniques for buying a house can be adapted and applied to virtually any purchase. Negotiation principles are essentially universal, and there's no reason to limit their application unless they're inappropriate in a specific circumstance.

Readers expect to see examples of actual negotiations they can relate to in order to enhance their knowledge and understanding of this subject. Ideally, I'd share some of the ones I did while working in aerospace, but that's impossible for two reasons. First, they were too complex and time-consuming for me to adequately explain and diagnose in the space available in this book. Second, security classification requirements prevent me from discussing them except in very general terms.

I recognize that some of your negotiations may be more stressful and complicated than the examples I'll introduce from my personal life. You might wonder if my fundamental principles would work in a relatively simplistic scenario but not as successfully when negotiating a convoluted labyrinth of prices, deliveries, incentives, warranties, terms, and conditions. I've been there, and it can be daunting to tie everything together and reach a favorable conclusion.

I employ the same principles regardless of the size and complexity of the subject matter. My overall strategy and tactics remain consistent and don't fluctuate as a function of who or what I'm dealing with. I only alter my approach if some highly unusual and unpredictable circumstance makes it impossible for me to proceed otherwise. My examples are simple and easy to understand, but the top-line takeaways are just as crucial to your success.

I never walk into a negotiation thinking I have the slightest chance of not getting what I want. I walk in believing I'm better equipped than everyone else in the room, and figuratively speaking, I'll add them to the landscape littered with the bodies of people I've taken on in negotiations over the past four decades. I'm prepared, I'm confident, and I'm not there to compromise. I'll defeat the other party by whatever legal and ethical means necessary. I will never apologize for defending my position and aggressively pursuing my objectives while always remembering that psychological warfare works better than actual combat in the negotiating room.

Later in this book, I detail the vital qualities of a successful negotiator. It starts with attitude and presence and progresses from there. So please forgive me if my opening line about the preeminence of this book seemed overly presumptuous. It's intended to encapsulate and cement a pivotal concept in your mind that will reap huge rewards if you favorably consider the advice presented in this book. To be a good negotiator, you must think like, act like, talk like, and believe you're a good negotiator.

In the Beginning

After leaving a blossoming career in broadcast radio, my father opened an auction business that sold used items he bought for resale and items sold for other people on consignment. He took a percentage of all the consignments that moved through his auction barn. My brothers and I worked as runners in his auctions from a very early age. We brought sold items to the buyers and collected the money. We learned many valuable business lessons and witnessed how the give-and-take of the bidding process determined market values. I clearly remember my father telling us that something is worth what someone else is willing and able to pay for it—nothing more and nothing less. I've always remembered that when entrenched in a tough negotiation with no end in sight.

There were always dealers at the auctions who were hoping to buy on the cheap and resell at higher prices in the future. Some owned antique shops, while others sold at flea markets and swap meets. Watching them compete against each other during the bidding was a priceless education. I observed their wheeling and dealing tactics firsthand without having my own money on the line. I recognized that psychology and emotion played a significant role in how high they were willing to bid and when they'd decide to stop bidding. Those lessons were invaluable as a contract negotiator and program manager in my later years.

My first memory of negotiation was with my father when he took me to look at an antique chest he was interested in buying. I was a young boy and hadn't started school yet. At that time, I had two older brothers in school and one younger brother who was too young to go on such an expedition. Getting me out of the house for several hours made it slightly easier for my mother to care for the baby.

In those days, we referred to antique furniture as used furniture. It's hard to imagine this today, but new furniture back then was often more expensive than handcrafted furniture made 200 years earlier. The idea of bringing old furniture into your home and using it was foreign to some people, but not to my parents, who couldn't afford new furniture. My father didn't buy used furniture as an investment because there was little expectation that it would significantly appreciate in value. The concept of collecting antiques as we know it today didn't yet exist on a wide scale. He focused on finding furniture we could clean up, refinish if necessary, and use in our home. Little did we know that the items he bought would explode in value over the next several decades.

We headed to Acton, Maine, to look at a Chippendale maple chest-on-chest circa 1760. London cabinetmaker Thomas Chippendale provided the design inspiration for the American-made furniture named after him. It's distinguishable by its dark woods and distinctive styling of the legs and feet. The chest was an exquisite example of American craftsmanship, handed down in the same family for generations. The top section had five graduated drawers with brass pulls, and the base section had three large drawers with brass pulls. It was beautifully dovetailed and perfectly sized and proportioned. In my father's words, it was a "gem" of a find, and he wouldn't leave without it.

What was this exquisite chest worth? Before answering that question, let's put this transaction in perspective. At that time, there were no pricing guides for antique furniture, and you couldn't jump on the internet and do a quick search for similar sales. Furniture like this rarely changed hands, and most families were reluctant to part with cherished heirlooms. Information regarding market values for used furniture at that time was sparse. The best way to find out what it was worth was to put it up for sale in a public auction and see what it would bring, but my father didn't want that to happen and risk losing it to a bidder who could afford to push up the price.

I don't recall what was said to get to the bottom line, but the horse-trading went back and forth for some time. I remember my father handing over $100, which seemed like all the money in the world to me. Years later, he told me it was half what they wanted, and he knew it was worth at least that much. He also told me only a fool pays the asking price because people always ask for more than they think they can get. That's a fundamental lesson about human nature that I never forgot, and it works both ways. Whether you're the buyer or seller, remember that people have preconceived notions and perceptions that aren't easily overcome. Plan accordingly before making or accepting an offer.

Fast forward to today, and that 260+ year-old chest occupies a prime spot in my home. What's it worth now compared to what my father paid for it? It's difficult to assess since chests like this are so rare, each one is unique, and very few ever come up for sale. If I decide to sell it, I'll get well over a hundred bucks, even after adjusting for inflation.

My father made a name for himself across the country as an auctioneer and antiques appraiser and was considered an expert in his field. Before *Antiques Roadshow* appeared on American airwaves in 1997, he hosted the *Antiques* television show originally broadcast on National Educational Television (NET), which preceded the Public Broadcasting Service (PBS). The show premiered in 1963 and continued its association with NET and PBS until 1985. He also authored seven books on antiques and, in 1986, became the first New England auctioneer inducted into the National Auctioneers Association Hall of Fame.

How I Learned the Ropes

----- ----- ----- ----- ----- ----- ----- ----- ----- ----- ----- ----- -----

After graduating from USAFA, my first assignment as a second lieutenant was to the Northrop Corporation Air Force Plant Representative Office (AFPRO) in Hawthorne, California. Fans of sixties rock 'n' roll music might recognize Hawthorne as the hometown of the three Wilson brothers and their band, originally known as the Pendletones. The surf uniform of the day consisted of khakis with plaid Pendleton flannel shirts worn over white tee shirts.

Their house, located at 3701 West 119th Street, was within easy walking distance of the Northrop plant. I met several employees who grew up watching them play in their garage along with their cousin Mike Love and friend David Marks, who lived across the street. Others joined the band, and when they started recording songs, an executive from their first record company renamed them the Beach Boys.

Many years later, the construction of the I-105 Glenn Anderson Freeway required the demolition of the house. The roadway is better known to locals as the Century Freeway since it parallels Century Boulevard. The western ends of both roadways terminate at the Los Angeles International Airport. Portions of the movie *Speed* were filmed at various points along the route before opening the new freeway to traffic.

The now vacant Wilson family homesite was designated as California State Historic Landmark No. 1041 by the California State Historic Resources Commission. A monument accessible to the public was constructed to honor the band and is not far from the airport. The one and only Dick Clark was a driving force in making this monument a reality.

When I arrived for duty at the Northrop AFPRO, I negotiated foreign military sales contracts for the F-5E International Fighter. This lightweight, twin-engine jet fighter was the mainstay of the Northrop Aircraft Division at the time, with sales going to foreign countries worldwide. There was also a significant spare parts procurement contract that accompanied the fighter sales.

I next served as a member of a six-man team that monitored the YF-17 air combat fighter development in support of the Aeronautical Systems Division at Wright-Patterson Air Force Base. I witnessed the first flight of the prototype at Edwards Air Force Base. This aircraft was in a head-to-head competition with the General Dynamics YF-16 for a full-scale production contract with the U.S. Air Force. The winner would likely join the air forces of allied countries that needed near-term replacements for their F-5s. As a contract administrator, I negotiated with Northrop on behalf of the Air Force and its allied customers.

When the YF-17 lost to the YF-16 in the Air Force lightweight fighter competition, the Navy became interested in the YF-17 to supplement the bigger and more expensive F-14 Tomcat. Unlike the YF-16, the YF-17 featured twin engines and was more suitable as a fighter/bomber for aircraft carrier deployments. The Navy's modified, carrier-based version was redesignated as the F/A-18 Hornet.

My second assignment as a first lieutenant and captain was to the Space and Missile Systems Organization (SAMSO) in El Segundo, California. As a project officer in a system program office (SPO), I was responsible for budget management, financial planning, and contract negotiations for multiple defense satellite contracts for the Air Force and the Navy.

After leaving military active duty, I joined the private aerospace industry as a business, contracts, and program manager for classified defense satellite programs. Much of my work involved creating and presenting executive briefings, negotiation strategies, and new business plans for critical, high-technology programs. I led several teams that negotiated over $4 billion in contracts, many of which were complex procurements involving long-range cost, schedule, and performance incentives. Some of these negotiations took months to complete, and that experience deep in the trenches formed the cornerstone for this book.

I'm confident you'll benefit from my firsthand experience on the front lines, where I thoroughly tested my tactics and strategies. I discuss my personal negotiations and what I did to maximize results and achieve my goals. I practice what I preach, and I know it works.

Negotiation Basics

-- -- -- -- -- -- -- -- -- -- -- -- -- -- -- -- --

Merriam-*Webster* defines "negotiate" as follows: "to confer with another so as to arrive at the settlement of some matter" and "to arrange for or bring about through conference, discussion, and compromise." Interestingly, there's no mention of agreement on a price. The definition ignores the common perception that negotiations are primarily a numbers game. The stereotypical depiction includes one or more people on opposite sides of a table debating over the price of an object. One side represents the buyer, and the other side represents the seller.

The stereotypical negotiation constitutes a tiny fraction of the negotiations taking place around the clock. Most of us don't realize when they're taking place and wouldn't necessarily call them negotiations. Many things we do daily involve negotiation to some extent, and most often, they have nothing to do with price. These are just a few examples of everyday negotiations.

- Deciding where your group will go for lunch
- Place and time for a meeting
- Selecting a new computer network
- What's for dinner tonight
- Which movie to see this weekend
- How late your child can stay up

- **Where to go on vacation**
- **Whether or not to adopt a new pet**

All of these involve give-and-take to some degree, which lies at the heart of most negotiations. Apart from the business world, negotiation is rarely about price. Whenever possible, it should be the last thing you discuss. Before you can agree on a price, the scope, schedule, and terms and conditions of what is being negotiated need to be nailed down.

Assume you're a company purchaser, and you've been asked to buy a new company car. You go to the local dealer and place an order for the year, make, model, and color you want, along with the optional equipment needed. Both you and the dealer sign a contract that spells out the details. You call a week later to find out the status of your order, and you're told it will be eight months before the car is delivered.

Your boss is expecting the car now. What can you do? You're stuck unless you specified a delivery date or not-later-than date in the contract. You can complain to the dealer, but the dealer is not obligated to cancel the contract and allow you to buy a different car. If you had specified your need date in writing, the dealer would have either agreed to it or not signed the contract. You would have understood on the spot whether this dealer could meet all your requirements.

Had you known the delivery was eight months away, you could have used that fact as leverage to negotiate a lower price. Once you signed the contract, however, that leverage vanished. You don't get a do-over to retrace time and correct oversights that would have saved you money.

The lesson learned is to ensure that every term and condition you want enforced is included in the written contract. If the dealer provides verbal assurances regarding any of those elements, add them to the contract if they're relevant to your purchase. If you ever land in court because of a dispute regarding the car, any verbal agreements or understandings will be overridden by the written contract—the contract rules.

Resolve all outstanding issues before you make or accept any offers in a negotiation. In the world of contracts, this is called a "meeting of the minds." Avoid shaking hands on a deal and finding out later that key provisions that would have influenced the final price should have been discussed.

These are the basics of contract formation that will be covered in more detail later in this book.

- **Offer**
- **Acceptance**
- **Consideration**
- **Mutual assent**
- **Legal capacity**

The important point to remember when you're nearing an agreement is that you have genuine mutual assent on all relevant provisions, not just the price.

My Kind of Negotiator

Negotiating is a learnable skill, but it helps if you already possess certain traits and talents that are difficult to teach. There are many that I'll cover, but the two most important are the ability to read and persuade people.

Reading people is my way of describing the capability to discern what they're thinking and predict what they'll do in reaction to your statements and actions. We can't read minds, but we can evaluate how and why people react through their body language and speech patterns and analyze what they say and how they say it. You want to know what motivates them and observe their behavioral patterns, feelings, concerns, opinions, and overall personality. You might call this getting a sense of people and what makes them tick.

When looking for clues about what you're up against, use every technique and method available to size up your opponent. Most people behave and operate on two distinct levels. The first is what is observable on the surface and is manifested by how they look, talk, act, and react. The second is the underlying mental and emotional makeup that drives and propels that behavior. It's common for people to put on a front when you first meet. Negotiators must be able to see through that and move quickly to the second level. If you can develop the ability to read people effectively, you've mastered what I consider the number one negotiating skill.

The second component of my top two skills is the ability to persuade people. I've observed several individuals who possess an inborn talent to talk their way into and out of anything virtually at will. Whenever I think of great salesmen, one of the first names that comes to mind is the late Billy Mays. While I don't necessarily recommend his pitchman style in a negotiation setting, his charm, enthusiasm, charisma, and product knowledge are all positive qualities that endeared him to his legion of fans. Various companies sought his services to exploit the personal attributes that made him so effective. Videos of Billy in action are available on the internet.

The art of persuasion can be learned, but not in a classroom. Two quotes about diplomacy capture the flavor of the persuasive art form. "Diplomacy is the art of telling people to go to hell in such a way that they ask for directions." "Diplomacy is the art of letting someone else have your way." Both quotes have multiple attributions, encapsulating an approach radically different from the stereotypical "tough guy" negotiator. Persuasion usually works better than coercion, and assertiveness is better than aggression. I have nothing to gain by pounding the other party into submission. I aim to convince them that our deal is their best possible outcome.

I look for several qualities in a skilled negotiator, and I'll elaborate on them in no particular order.

Ideally, you'll have an abundance of rock-solid, real-world negotiating experience behind you. Early in my career, I had the opportunity to work in procurement at two Air Force units in southern California. My second assignment at SAMSO was to a satellite SPO under the command of Colonel Forrest McCartney (whose signature graces the back cover of this book). He was a brilliant strategist and tactician, and watching him in action was more rewarding than a master's degree in program management. I elaborate on this experience in the chapter titled "Great Leaders Negotiate." Both assignments offered multiple opportunities to negotiate high dollar-value contracts for fighter aircraft and communication satellites. One solid advantage enjoyed by young military officers is that they gain valuable experience at a relatively young age. I took full advantage of this experience during my time on active duty.

Confidence in yourself is crucial. Even if you're experiencing some anxiety and uncertainty about a situation, the key is to project confidence at all times. As a young child, my father always told me if an untrained dog sensed you were afraid, it was more likely to attack and bite you. Back in those days, there were no leash laws where I lived, so dogs roamed freely throughout our neighborhood. Walking to school was a challenging adventure because my path crossed with menacing dogs continually threatening my safety. I tried to keep my fear in check and pretend I owned my route, and the dogs left me alone.

Henry Ford once said, "Whether you believe you can do a thing or not, you are right." His point was that positive and negative thinking are often at war, and only you can pick sides. When asked if he stood to lose a large amount of money if his decisions went wrong, he said he never thought about things going wrong. He warned never to let yourself believe you can fail, even for a second. That sentiment was echoed many years later during the movie *Apollo 13*. While NASA flight director Gene Kranz never actually said, "Failure is not an option," it became the movie's tagline and mantra for the team that orchestrated the safe return of the three astronauts onboard the spacecraft. In the real-life drama that unfolded in April 1970, Kranz ensured that everyone on his team understood those men would not be lost on his watch.

We're all human. If you find your confidence slipping amid a heated negotiation, buckle up and fake it. What counts is what you project to the opposition. Perception is everything. Don't hesitate to take a break for a few minutes, an hour, or the rest of the day. If you're part of a negotiating team, take time to caucus, regroup, and rethink your strategy. Don't let them beat you because of a weak moment. We've all experienced those moments, but it won't defeat you if you're prepared to deal with it. Act like you own the place and are not inclined to take prisoners.

Credibility is something you earn over time by demonstrating you know what you're talking about and can back it up. Developing a reputation as a credible person who stands by their convictions gives you leverage when you otherwise might not have any. Consistency is key. If you're in a position where bluffing is necessary to close a deal, you're more likely to pull it off if you've built up a level of credibility that makes the other party think very hard before calling your bluff. You want them to presume their risk outweighs the expected reward.

"Patience is a virtue" is an oft-quoted line whose origin is hard to pin down, and it's a quality that routinely goes against our instincts. We live in times dominated by fast-food restaurants and the search for instant gratification. Those impulses must be controlled and set aside during a negotiation. Working to a deadline gives the other party tremendous leverage, so avoid suggesting or implying that you must conclude negotiations quickly. If you're under pressure to finish by a specific date, only disclose that to the other party if you're prepared to walk away if it doesn't happen. I'd tell the other party you're ready to walk to flip the leverage back in your court. The key is to maintain your persistence while remaining patient.

I've discovered through personal experience that negotiators from foreign countries are generally more patient than Americans. A fast-food mentality can cost you money if you're not prepared to outlast the other side, regardless of how frustrated you are that negotiations are dragging on without progress. Delaying progress is a common tactic when there's little leverage to rely on. The hope is that one side will eventually tire to the point where they unwillingly make concessions to close the deal. Avoid being mired in this position.

If you become involved in international negotiations, you'll soon realize the tactics and strategies you've relied on in the past have suddenly lost some of their effectiveness. Cultural differences make it more challenging to read the other party because your educational background and life experiences may have little in common. Since the ability to read people is at the top of my list of critical attributes, you need to find other ways to get inside their heads. I acknowledge this is easier said than done. Begin with the assumption that they don't think like you do and likely don't share your priorities. Listen closely, don't take anything for granted, and keep an open mind. The more you learn about them, the better prepared you'll be to devise a uniquely potent negotiating plan.

Communication skills are indispensable in many ways. It's your responsibility to ensure the other party understands the basis for your position and your evaluation of theirs. This understanding is a critical component of the early stages of a negotiation, especially before establishing an anchor or benchmark position. An anchor will only hold significant weight if it has sound logic and supporting rationale backing it up.

Negotiation involves a lot of talking or what might be called give-and-take as both parties jockey for position. After exchanging the introductory niceties and pleasantries, I only talk if I have some-thing worth saying that's integral to the negotiation. As a general rule, it's more important to know when not to talk as it is to talk. If the other party rambles on and on about this and that, I usually let them hold the floor for as long as they like. Invariably, they'll let something slip that I'll use against them later. Then they learn a lesson they hope not to forget, summarized in this quote attributed to Abraham Lincoln, Mark Twain, and others: "Better to remain silent and be thought a fool than to speak and to remove all doubt."

Listen carefully to everything they say, and let them talk until the cows come home. Make mental notes of the conversation and write down any significant points. Listening is often far more important and productive than anything you might say in response. Dr. Stephen Covey, a well-known author and educator, frequently emphasized the crucial difference between hearing and listening. The distinction he makes is vital in the context of a negotiation that involves continuous give-and-take. He took that construct a step further when he said, "Most people do not listen with the intent to understand; they listen with the intent to reply." Think about it. Isn't that observation at the heart of almost every argument you've ever had?

If you doubt Covey's potent observation, tune in to any political debates between opposing parties. They're hearing each other, but they don't care what the other is saying and display little desire to understand the basis for their opinions. Instead, their brains are churning overtime to prepare to reply with a knockout blow. The response is everything. Understanding their respective positions is low on the priority list, regardless of how good they are at pretending otherwise.

Common sense and intuition play a prominent role, but many people tend to discount or ignore their instincts in the moment's emotion. The best salesmen will steer you in their direction by suppressing what your gut is telling you. They accomplish this through differing means that reflect your feelings and desire to be fair and reasonable. Being fair and reasonable is the last thing I'm worried about when buying a car. I'm not there to convince anyone to be my new friend or win a popularity contest. I'm there to buy the most car for the least amount of money.

Superior analytical skills provide a massive advantage because they allow you to see through the "noise" and get to the heart of what's driving the other party's position. They're trying to take money out of your pocket and deposit it in theirs, and you have to be able to dissect what they're doing to counteract potential damage to your position. Critical thinking skills and deductive reasoning allow you to penetrate their arguments and formulate your future strategy. You should be thinking constantly and doing it on the fly.

It helps if you have a good logic path to rapidly process information flow and connect the dots as you go.

I'm using "connect the dots" as a metaphor for demonstrating the ability to immerse yourself in details while keeping your eye on the big picture. When swamped with complicated data, it's critical to focus on the salient and most relevant aspects and determine how those contribute to or detract from your negotiation strategy. Unless you're fortunate, the other party isn't going to draw a roadmap or spell it out for you. Be prepared to make sense of something that may not make sense on the surface. A coherent, logical thought process will help you analyze data and come to reasoned conclusions based on verifiable facts.

A tough, protracted negotiation can be a very taxing experience that will test your resolve and endurance. It's understandable why some people will ultimately make concessions to reach closure, even if it means paying more than they otherwise would. It takes discipline, self-control, and an iron gut to stand your ground while enduring unrelenting assault by someone who's determined not to back down and give you what you want. You need to know there's an excellent chance they feel the same way you do, and they're looking for the slightest crack in your armor to plant the final blow. There's no reason to lose this game of chicken, but you have to believe in your strategy to win it. Act like you'll win, and never let the other side think for one second that you'll accept defeat.

It's important to anticipate your opponent's actions as the negotiation progresses and develop the ability to predict their moves within a narrow range of options. Take everything you know up to that point and ask yourself what you would do if you were in their shoes. Second-guess your opponent and keep him guessing.

There's no blueprint for strategies and tactics that will work in every negotiation. Therefore, no plan will be flawless. However, you'll be in a much better position to think and act on the fly if you've prepared a few options and solutions for whatever's thrown at you. Flexibility and adaptability are key. Create the perception that you're ready even when you aren't. Whatever you do, don't panic. The other side will see that as a glowing sign of weakness.

A healthy dose of skepticism and cynicism is a valuable asset that helps to avoid surprises. Everything is not always as it appears on the surface, so prepare yourself to question and challenge purported facts and assumptions relied on by the other party. When things don't add up or make sense, your instincts and intuition are your best friends, so never ignore what they tell you. Assume nothing and take nothing at face value. Curiosity may have killed the cat, but you need to turn that idiom on its head in negotiations where there's no place for the timid and fainthearted.

When it comes to negotiation skills, what does not impress me? You've got a Master of Business Administration degree from Harvard or a Juris Doctor degree from Yale, and you've read ten books written by negotiation "experts" who've never been in the trenches of a complex negotiation worth millions of dollars that takes months to complete. What some would call "book smarts" aren't worth much and don't automatically make you a good negotiator.

I alternately fear and respect negotiators possessing the qualities outlined in this chapter, and I've come up against some of the best. I don't know where they went to college or if they have a college degree. It never mattered. What counted was their judgment, street smarts, decision-making skills, and ability to think from the top down and the bottom up. They never let the stress and intense pressure of a high-stakes negotiation affect their demeanor, professionalism, or ability to drive the hardest bargain imaginable. I'd describe them as cutthroat negotiators, but only to compliment their ability to consistently present formidable obstacles to getting what I wanted.

Negotiation Mindset

During six of the best minutes ever put on film, George C. Scott (as General George S. Patton), in a speech to his men of the Third Army, says, "Now, I want you to remember that no bastard ever won a war by dying for his country. He won it by making the other poor dumb bastard die for his country." That mindset established Patton as one of the greatest field generals in the history of warfare. While I'd never equate a negotiation to a war, the self-confidence to prevail over the opposition is crucial to success. Patton knew that instinctively and knew his men had to believe it as much as he did.

Negotiation involves an entirely different form of confrontation. If you already experience enough conflict in your everyday life, are you inclined to intentionally create more of it? You may have no choice, especially if you're a small business owner who feels the constant pressure to negotiate daily. Their livelihood depends on it. If they don't know how to deal with it, they either learn quickly or get swallowed up by a relentless system that doesn't tolerate failure. The survival of your business depends on your ability to deal with whatever problems you encounter. That reality is a huge motivator to push you into doing whatever it takes to succeed.

My father was a small businessman and avoided confrontation like the plague. As I got older, I sensed that the people he did business with took advantage of him, which inevitably cost him money. There were many times when he should have taken a firmer stand when that occurred, but he treated it as a cost of doing business. His operating theory was that whatever he lost on one deal, he'd more than make back on the next. I don't know if that ever happened, but it worked for him. His methods also kept his stress levels to a minimum and contributed to a healthier life.

A successful negotiator projects self-confidence and a willingness to dive into disputed issues to explore and uncover solutions. If you're timid or unsure of yourself, the other party will immediately notice and use that to their advantage. You can't afford to put yourself in that position. Even if it's just an act, you must act the part. You always want them to see someone knowledgeable about the subject matter, prepared to defend your position, and operating at the top of your game.

I believe in the power of positive thinking and its ability to influence actual results. One of the best documented examples of this phenomenon occurs during the testing of new drugs. Known as the "placebo effect," it demonstrates that the mind can be a powerful healing tool when you don't know if your medicine is real or fake. Under the right circumstances, the brain convinces your body that the placebo is the real thing and performs as well or better than the actual drug. That's evidence of positive thinking taken to the next level, where you believe what you're doing will genuinely work. A placebo won't cure you of anything, but it can alter symptoms controlled by the brain, such as pain. Sometimes, simply changing the perception of how much pain you feel can be deemed a success.

The weapons arsenal of good negotiators includes hefty doses of positive thinking and an optimistic outlook for achieving goals. While this seems obvious, there's no shortage of people who enter negotiations as defeatists for one reason or another. Perhaps they've already resigned themselves to thinking their negotiating position is weak, or the other party has superior leverage that will be difficult to overcome. That kind of thinking will likely sink you faster than the Titanic striking an iceberg in the North Atlantic.

In the 1980s, William Usery, appointed by the Secretary of Labor, mediated the dispute between the United Mine Workers of America and the Pittston Coal Company. While attempting to find a resolution, he told a story about two kids, one a pessimist and the other an optimist. The adults put the pessimist in a room full of fantastic toys and put the optimist in a room full of horse manure. Later, they returned to see who was the happiest.

The pessimist sat in the middle of the fantastic toys, crying. He feared that playing with the toys would break them or someone would take them away. The optimist played happily with the manure, throwing it around the room and excitedly digging through it. When asked why he was so thrilled with the manure, he said, "There's got to be a pony around here somewhere!"

While that story overdramatizes the point, it illustrates how attitude alone creates a stark difference in one's perception of their surroundings. A negative attitude will almost certainly be detected by the other party in a negotiation and exploited to your detriment. While having uncertainties and doubts about your chances is expected, the key is to conceal them from all negotiation participants, including your team members.

We've all experienced the three stages of desire: I want it, I need it, and I can't live without it. As a buyer, always enter negotiations with the "I want it" mindset, which is purely common sense. If the seller discerns that you can't live without the item he's selling, that's all the leverage he needs to hold firm on his price or start even higher. Needing it gives him less leverage, but it's still an advantage you don't want to give away for nothing. Don't fall in love with anything you're buying. If you ever do, hide your emotion from the seller. To get what you want, negotiate like it's about something other than what you want.

Some people are cut out to be good negotiators, and people routinely do it only because they must. Their reluctance to negotiate often persists even when they have the upper hand. Everyday life is a continuing series of negotiations at home, work, school, or wherever life takes you and often puts you in the uncomfortable position of squaring off with the unavoidable. We do it because we have no choice. My goal is to put you in the best position possible to conquer some of that anxiety and help you do it to the best of your ability.

Psychology 101

I took a psychology course in college as a core curriculum requirement. We had one book that was the basis for the course instruction, and we were assigned reading lessons for each class. After the first few chapters, I put the book away and never touched it again. As a result of what I'd read, I found myself overanalyzing everything I did. Spontaneity and creativity sailed out the window in favor of constant self-analysis and reflective self-evaluation. I couldn't take it, and it was driving me crazy.

The instructor encouraged us to ask why we did or didn't do certain things and psychoanalyze every aspect of our behavior. I found this process so inherently destructive that I focused all my energy on passing the course without reading, studying, or learning anything. I succeeded in getting a "B" only because I passed the tests using simple logic, deductive reasoning, and common sense, all essential qualities of a successful negotiator. I delved into those qualities and many others in the prior chapter titled "My Kind of Negotiator."

The course reminded me of the comprehensive physical examination I underwent before my academy appointment. Part of the exam included a psychological evaluation by a colonel assigned to the Air Force base medical facility. I assume he had a degree in psychiatry or psychology, although I don't remember him introducing himself as such.

Since this was the last phase of the two-day exam process, I was already mentally and physically exhausted. I'm sure the scheduling was intentional. The Air Force wanted to see how well we'd withstand the pressure of an intense screening process designed to irritate, aggravate, and provoke us to react emotionally and antagonistically. They had driven us to a vulnerable position, and now the colonel was determined to find out how mentally tough we were.

I didn't know it then, but the first year at the academy would be the most physically and mentally demanding time of my life. The countless challenges thrown at the new cadets were constant, and the unmistakable purpose of the psych eval was to weed out those who wouldn't meet the mental challenge that awaited us. As it turned out, about 40% of my entering class never made it to graduation for various reasons, and most of them left during the first few months of basic training and the balance of that first year.

The colonel was slick and sneaky, asking me how I would react to various situations and hypotheticals. He got my attention when he asked if I was closer to my father or mother. I told him I was close to both and didn't think it was his business. Then he asked if I was a momma's boy and had started shaving yet. I couldn't help but start laughing, which wasn't the reaction he expected. He asked what was so funny, and I said that he was proof positive that the only people on this planet who need the services of a psychiatrist are other psychiatrists. When he broke out laughing, I knew the session was over. He didn't say another word, but I passed without ever being subjected to the tough part to come.

I had yet to learn how relevant the training I received at the academy would be to negotiating effectively later in my career. We learned how to deal with tremendous stress and pressure while making critical decisions with minimal information on which to base those decisions. While lives are not in jeopardy in a negotiation, the psychological forces at work are always present and should never be discounted.

While we often think of bluffing as being associated with card games like poker, it's also a vital ingredient of your negotiation arsenal. The risks are much higher if you consistently negotiate multimillion-dollar contracts and do it with company money.

The ability to bluff depends on many things, but I'd start with personal credibility. If you negotiate regularly with the same people, you'll develop a reputation that precedes you. The burden is on you to ensure your reputation is respected. Some negotiators might also say they want to be feared, but I'd use a different word than fear. I prefer they exhibit deep concern and apprehension about the strategies and tactics I'll use to dismantle their negotiating position.

For a bluff to work, you need the other party to trust you, even though it would be a mistake if they did. The idea, of course, is to ensure they never find out it was a bluff. Depending on house rules, when you bluff in poker, you usually don't expose your cards when all the other players have folded their hands.

The setup is a flexible process adapted to the specific circumstances of your negotiation. One of the ways to build credibility is to be a good listener, even if you're only pretending to be one. You want to assure the other side that you're taking them seriously and will consider everything they say relevant to the outcome. Listening more than talking also reduces the risk of saying something you wish you could take back later.

Only attempt a bluff once you're reasonably sure you've gained the other side's confidence. To accomplish this, you must exude confidence through your body language, what you say, and how you say it. Courtesy, charm, and wardrobe go a long way, as does conveying an air of authority by being prepared with an overall execution strategy.

If the other side senses you know precisely what you're doing, it doesn't matter whether you actually do or not. Fake it if you have to. Trickery is a useful tactic to exploit, but you'll only get away with it if you've already established a good measure of credibility and confidence. You'll be in a far stronger position to bluff if the other side believes they're starting to lose the credibility battle.

I recommend bluffing in a negotiation only when you believe it's necessary and properly set up with a reasonable chance of success. The downside risk is catastrophic if the other side calls your bluff.

Former President Calvin Coolidge had a legendary and well-earned reputation for not talking much and was often called "Silent Cal" in the media. Channing Cox, who succeeded Coolidge as governor of Massachusetts, had a meeting scheduled with the president at 11:00 a.m. one day. He arrived early at the White House and was ushered into the Oval Office precisely on time. Cox couldn't believe it since he often worked into the night due to meetings that constantly went overtime, and was shocked that the leader of the free world was able to see him at the exact time as scheduled. Cox told the president that when people came to his office, they talked and talked and talked, and he could never get rid of them. "Your problem, governor," said Coolidge, "is that you talk back."

Coolidge understood the old axiom that silence can be golden. Analyzing that maxim in the context of a negotiation, if the other side believes they've been heard and understood, they're far more likely to listen to you. Another aspect of this approach is that statements precipitate resistance, while questions induce acquiescence, especially during the early stages of the negotiation.

Sometimes, Coolidge exhibited his reticence in unexpected and humorous ways. One evening, the first family hosted a dinner at the White House. Before taking her seat next to Coolidge, an invited guest made a bet with another guest that she could get the president to talk to her. After sitting down, she told him about her bet that she would get more than two words out of him. He looked directly at her and without missing a beat replied, "You lose."

A recounting of this story occurred at the 1924 Associated Press luncheon at the Waldorf Astoria Hotel when Coolidge was introduced as the featured speaker. Before delivering his prepared remarks, the president casually dismissed the story as an unfounded "rumor." However, many years later this story, along with several others, was confirmed by his son John during a radio interview with my father.

A skilled negotiator knows when to shut his mouth and is delighted when the other side is willing to fill every second of dead air. There's no payoff to acting like you're the most intelligent person in the room. I'd rather sit back and wait for the unforced errors to accumulate as they attempt to impress me with their thoroughness and objectivity. The gift of gab is not an asset in a contentious negotiation where both sides battle for higher ground and superior leverage.

If you feel compelled to talk because you want to temporarily shut them down, recount a summary of what they've been telling you as a way of confirming their bias. It also places them in a safe zone where they feel more comfortable expressing their desire to forge a resolution and clarify their true thoughts and feelings. They'll be far more likely to expose valuable information when they know you're genuinely interested and listening to their position. Once you establish a connection, a real conversation ensues, demonstrating you understand their concerns. Put yourself in their shoes and acknowledge their perspective in a nonthreatening way.

Never underestimate the power of observation. I constantly detect verbal and nonverbal cues validating the other party's emotional state. Body language is crucial because it's a dead giveaway for the average person struggling to suppress their emotions. People are most vulnerable when you first meet, so pay particular attention to how they act and react. They tend to let their guard down before the official business gets underway. Nothing happened yet that would cause them to distrust or alienate you. How they interact during breaks and caucuses can also be revealing.

Draw a bright line between their psychological state and the problem you're attempting to solve. It's difficult to do when their emotions are entangled in a disagreement, such as a divorce proceeding. Depending on the circumstances, sometimes it's better to let the lawyers duke it out with no one else in the room.

Refrain from believing the other party always thinks like you do or is even capable of what you'd consider rational, logical thought. It's pure coincidence if their goals and aspirations mirror yours. They usually don't, and pretending they do is a mistake. Once you've opened the door to unfiltered connectivity, you'll be in a much better position to disagree without being disagreeable later on. The key is building rapport and establishing trust before attempting to resolve actual conflicts.

Declarative statements contradicting the other party's position may be perceived as threatening and put them on the defensive, thus likely reducing their receptiveness to your position. The best way to diffuse your differences is to ask intelligent questions about their position that demonstrate your understanding, but not necessarily your agreement, with what they're saying. Questions are inclusive and encourage others to expose their weaknesses. That's precisely your mission.

It's sometimes possible to elicit responses to questions that give you the solution you seek. While this may seem like a long shot, remember you're attempting to get a genuine sense of what the other party wants. One way to do this is to ask generic questions for which there may be multiple possible answers. The idea is to get them thinking positively about finding common ground and a way to satisfy both sides. Such questions could include: "What can we do to bring our positions closer together?" or "How can we get from here to a successful conclusion?" You're not asking for numbers. Ask questions without boundaries to show them you're open to their ideas and suggestions. Avoid narrow questions that can be answered with "yes" or "no."

You're also setting the stage for what's to come by focusing on three main elements. First, consider multiple approaches as you advance and stay flexible. Second, keep it simple and don't lose sight of the big picture. Third, negotiate on the merits, principles, and mutual interests, not on individual positions. I can't overstate the importance of that last statement. It's tough to progress in a negotiation if you focus all your attention on your number versus their number. Both sides must be willing to engage on the merits of their respective positions and perform deep dives to identify common objectives and interests. Whenever possible, employ objective standards to identify commonalities between the two positions. This approach will help build the trust necessary to identify areas where you can find agreement.

While you can't unilaterally control a negotiation's progress, you can steer it by influencing the dialogue through questions and answers. Information gathered through these interactions will help influence the other party's behavior. The more you know, the better the chances you'll zero in on the optimal resolution.

The core of the art of negotiating is using all the tools at your disposal to influence and persuade the other party to have it your way. You want them to believe they played a crucial role in resolving your differences. Better yet, convince them it was their idea all along, which creates the illusion that they had far more control over the process than they actually did. How you go about this depends on who you're dealing with.

Start by searching for common ground at a personal level that all can relate to. Although we share a natural anxiety over what separates us, we're drawn together by mutual experiences. The similarity in our experiences can spawn a foundation of trust and open communication. You're more likely to guide the discussions and extract concessions when the other party reaches a comfort level consistent with their desire to move the negotiations forward.

We observe the impact of psychology on how goods for sale are priced, and this phenomenon opens the door to bargaining for something other than the sticker price. One facet of this is how people correlate price with quality. Sometimes, there's a direct correlation, but experience tells us that's not always true. A higher price does not always equate to better quality. A higher price could be a function of the seller increasing its margins, which means there's more for them to give back during a negotiation. Margin is often referred to as pad, reserve, cushion, and contingency. Your goal as a buyer is to negotiate that money out and keep it in your pocket rather than donating it to the seller.

As the seller, you have to know and understand the customer base you're trying to reach and how they react to different pricing methodologies. If you're targeting people who correlate price with quality and offer a high-quality product, price it accordingly. Just remember that their expectations will be high, and you need to meet them.

There are many classes of products where it's difficult to discern differences in quality, but the products have a wide range in prices. Is a $25 bottle of shampoo really five times better than another brand selling for $5? Many people think so, even though an analysis of the ingredients may reveal they're very similar. One of the reasons high-end retail stores charge more for their products is that customers expect it. That knowledge factors into every pricing decision they make.

There's an obvious reason why items are marked $9.99 instead of $10.00, and we all know what it is. Amazingly, the technique almost always works. Benjamin Franklin is credited with saying, "A penny saved is a penny earned." The point is well taken whether he said it or not. Even a negligible price difference can affect a potential buyer simply because of how the numbers look and sound. On the other hand, rounded numbers imply higher quality and impart an unwillingness to negotiate. While I don't advocate negotiating the price of inexpensive items, never assume that negotiation is off the table for anything you consider significantly overpriced, whether or not the seller seems willing.

The trick in retailing is to structure pricing that conveys quality and value and drives sales. That's far more art than science and requires a thorough understanding of the prospective customer base and competition.

Understanding how people think and what influences their perceptions and decision-making is essential. While details and facts are integral to the negotiation process, people are generally more persuaded by simplicity, repetition, emotion, and visual representations. They also tend to emphasize future trends over current conditions. Use these insights in developing your negotiation tactics and overall strategy.

If you find yourself mired in the weeds while debating a fine point, it's easy to get entrenched in the proverbial quicksand. The deeper you sink, the more difficult it becomes to extract yourself from a defensive position. Getting back on offense becomes paramount, and the sooner you do it, the better.

Steve Jobs found himself in a precarious position during the so-called iPhone 4 "antennaegate" public relations nightmare of 2010. The allegation was that the phone suffered from a design defect that induced a loss of signal strength and dropped calls when held in a certain way. A flawed antenna design allegedly caused the reception problems. The entire fiasco was a direct hit to Apple's reputation for high-quality products that the general public loved.

Jobs knew he had to change the focus on the specific issues and elevate the discussion above the sinkhole that was dragging his company down. The solution was to reframe the controversy into a reaffirmation of the general principles, in his eyes, that distinguished Apple from its competition. During a press conference called to address the situation, Jobs said, "You know, we're not perfect. We know that; you know that. And phones aren't perfect either. We want to make all of our users happy. If you don't know that about Apple, you don't know Apple. We love making our users happy." He promised free cases to all iPhone 4 users to alleviate the antenna issues.

He offered no apology and didn't acknowledge any mistakes. Isn't that what public relations experts typically recommend you do when you've been caught with your pants down with nothing to hold them up? Instead, Jobs switched the entire debate from what went wrong to what makes Apple customers some of the most loyal on the planet. Moreover, he did it with a brief statement that contained indisputable truths. He reframed and transformed the problem's context with unassailable principles impervious to reasonable disagreement.

In retrospect, this represented a masterful example of persuasion under trying circumstances. Jobs turned what could have been a marketing disaster into a positive reinforcement of Apple's commitment to its customers. In a negotiating sense, his actions ensured they would all get a fair deal and that Apple would continue to stand behind them no matter what. He executed and manipulated the levers of persuasion magnificently.

This technique is frequently employed in a political context. A good example is the U.S. invasion of Iraq in 2003, whose stated purpose was to find and eliminate weapons of mass destruction. The fear of another attack similar to that of 11 September 2001, was a powerful influence in rallying American public support. When no such weapons were found, the rationale for the invasion was reframed as the "Global War on Terrorism." Americans feared terrorism, so this was a means of capitalizing on that fear to justify further military action. This approach illustrates how enormous the consequences can be when the lives of our soldiers, sailors, and airmen are on the line.

A more recent example of reframing occurred shortly after the COVID-19 outbreak in the U.S. Lockdowns were mandated nationwide to "flatten the curve" of increasing hospitalizations due to the virus's rapid spread. Hospitals were reportedly being overrun and didn't have the requisite medical personnel, facilities, and ventilators to care for the explosion of new patients. The hospitalization curve was quickly flattened, but the lockdowns continued throughout the country.

In many states, lockdowns remained in effect for months and years after the curve had consistently dropped. The rationale for lockdowns beyond the original period was reframed as a means of reducing COVID-19 deaths, a justification that was markedly different than that used to gain initial public acceptance. Reframing is commonplace when the argument or rationale used to justify an action either fails to materialize or is overtaken by events. An alternative interpretation of reframing is that it ensures the ends justify the means by changing the rules in the middle of the game. If you keep moving the goalposts, you effectively reset the target to where you know you can hit it and still pretend that nothing materially changed.

While routine negotiations are nowhere near as consequential as pandemics or military action, proper framing is integral to effectual persuasion. The best trial attorneys almost universally possess this skill. Regardless of which side of the matter they're on, they must advocate for that side to the best of their ability. Presentation to the jury is paramount, and being a great story-teller is a monster advantage. The jury must perceive it through their eyes, and they can't get there through force or intimidation. Instead, it requires an appeal to reason, core values, and a commitment to an ideal.

How you frame an issue or argument can enormously impact how people react and respond. It's all about presentation, and the most skillful negotiators can elicit numerous responses to the same argument based solely on how they frame it. Mastering this skill enables you to create leverage in situations where it's difficult to find.

Contract Law Basics

Don't let the title of this chapter frighten you. You didn't buy a law book, and this book doesn't pretend to be one. However, you should have at least a basic understanding of contract law before engaging in consequential negotiations. Many negotiations are subsequently formalized into written agreements that both parties sign. Once that happens, there are ethical, performance, and financial obligations and commitments that are legally enforceable. Failure to comply with the agreement could result in a breach of contract litigation that can be costly and time-consuming. You can help avoid adverse consequences by understanding the how and why of contract formation.

A contract is an exchange of promises that constitute a binding agreement and define the obligations of all parties to it. An express contract is formed through an oral or written understanding of an agreement. The terms, conditions, and all the elements of a valid contract are expressly stated as part of the agreement.

An implied contract is assumed by the circumstances and actions of the parties or by the operation of law upon someone who receives a benefit he is not entitled to keep. For example, if you order and eat dinner at a restaurant, there is an implied contract to pay for it at the stated price before you leave. To deny the existence of a contract would unjustly enrich you at the expense of the restaurant owner.

There's a blueprint for creating an enforceable contract, and these are the key elements.

- **Offer / Counteroffer**
- **Acceptance**
- **Consideration**
- **Mutual assent (meeting of the minds)**
- **Legal capacity to enter into a contract**
- **Committed to writing, although not always legally required**

When these elements are satisfied, and there is a meeting of the minds on the terms of the agreement, the contract is enforceable in court or through arbitration. The consideration for the promise to perform is sufficient if a party: (1) agrees to do what they have no obligation to do, or (2) agrees not to do something they are entitled to do.

The offer and acceptance are straightforward concepts. Verbal offers are permitted unless both parties specify they must be in writing or if required by law. I always submit offers in writing, especially when significant amounts of money are involved, whether required or not. Sign and date them. While emails aren't typically signed, they're better than no writing. Committing these communications to some form of writing helps preclude arguments later on about who said what and when.

Keep notes containing the rationale for each offer and counteroffer you make. While there's no requirement to disclose the contents to the other party, they will prove invaluable should things go awry and you need to restart negotiations for any reason. Improving your skills includes benefiting from lessons learned and refining your approach and technique. If you work for a company or the government, those notes may be required to prepare a memorandum to document the negotiated outcome and complete the contract file.

An important fact is that a counteroffer acts as a rejection of an offer. Once a counteroffer is made, the prior offer is off the table and only open to acceptance if reinstated as a new offer. To illustrate the concept, let's assume you have a used car for sale with no established asking price. I offer you $10,000 for it. You counteroffer with $12,000. I reject that offer and provide no counteroffer. As I walk away, you decide to accept my initial $10,000 offer. It's too late. That offer was off the table once you made a counteroffer of $12,000. I can make a new offer of $10,000, which you could then accept, but I'm not compelled to do so.

In that example, if an offer by one party is eventually accepted, the basic elements of an agreement have been established. For a contract to stand up in court, there must be consideration on both sides of the accord. In a legal sense, consideration may take various forms, including money, goods, services, actions, and inactions. If I agree to buy the car for $10,000, the consideration offered by the seller is the car itself. My consideration could be a $10,000 check or cash, or I might agree to reroof the seller's house instead of payment. The point is that each party must give up something of real value to validate the contract.

There must also be mutual assent as to the substance and terms of the contract. For the sale of this car, it's a simple process to reach a meeting of the minds on the exchange of the car for payment or services. The vehicle identification number and description eliminate any confusion about what car is being sold, and the amount paid is unambiguously stated. Mutual assent can be more complicated if you're buying or selling a house, and contracts for real estate must be in writing to ensure clarity and comprehensiveness of the terms of sale. Contingencies such as financing and inspections are delineated to confirm that both parties agree to the same things for the same price.

The types of contracts required to be in writing vary by state, but the statute of frauds in most states applies to these categories.

- **Real property, including homes and land**
- **Contract value exceeds a stipulated maximum per state law**
- **Agreements related to marriage**

- Contracts lasting more than one year (including the lease of real property) or extending beyond the lifetime of the person performing under the contract
- Executor agrees to pay estate debts from personal funds
- Transfer of property in the event of the death of the performing party
- Promise to pay the debt of another

Verbal contracts are enforceable in court if they're not subject to the statute of frauds. I advise people to put everything in writing and have both parties sign and date it, even if it's a handwritten agreement on the back of an envelope. Formalize handwritten notes into a signed record as soon as possible. It's much easier to prove a case in court if there's a document you can produce to back up your claim. Even if a written agreement is not required, create one anyway, or you may later regret it.

If any party fails to perform according to the contract terms without a legal excuse, they have breached the contract. The performance failure must be significant enough to be material and cause the injured party to be relieved of further performance. If you suffer a breach by another party, you're entitled to compensation for the damages incurred, but you must take all reasonable actions to mitigate and minimize further damages. This duty applies even though you are not at fault.

Only negotiate with people with the legal capacity to enter into an enforceable contract. While there are certain exceptions, you must have reached the age of majority for a contract to be enforceable. You must also have the mental capacity to understand the effect and meaning of what you're agreeing to. If you have a cognitive impairment that prevents you from knowing you've consented to something, such a disability would constitute mental incapacitation to contract.

As a general rule, you can contract when voluntarily under the influence of drugs or alcohol. However, if you suspect the person you're dealing with is suffering from the effects of these substances, postpone any negotiations until they are of sound mind and can take full responsibility for their actions. Refrain from putting yourself in a position to take advantage of an unfortunate situation. It's not worth it to you in the long run and could damage your reputation and integrity in future negotiations. There are times when your reputation may be your only real leverage.

The many complexities of contract law extend far beyond the basic principles outlined here, so professional counsel may be appropriate depending on your circumstances. Remember Rule #1 when dealing with contracts: Carefully read the entire contract before signing it, especially the fine print. Once you affix your signature to that document, there's no going back to undo your fumbles, flubs, and blunders.

Preparation

Too many people enter negotiations without a well-conceived, viable plan. While they may think they have a plan, I couldn't agree more with Mike Tyson, who famously said, "Everybody has a plan until they get punched in the mouth [face]" before an upcoming fight against Evander Holyfield. There are several variations of what he said, including a similar statement made before an earlier fight against Tyrell Biggs. I could not verify the actual quote, but his point is indisputable. Another relevant quote, found in various forms and attributed to multiple people, is "No plan survives first contact with the enemy." One of my favorite quotes is from General George Patton: "A good plan, violently executed now, is better than a perfect plan next week."

I'd never equate a boxing match or military battle to a negotiation, but that doesn't take away from how integral planning is to achieving the results you want. I'm an amateur chess player, and I know many of the basic strategies and tactics of the game. I've always believed I'm not a better player because I've never developed the ability to plan several moves beyond the one I'm currently making. I need to play more to forge the strategic thinking required to elevate my game to the next level.

That shortcoming has yet to stop me from applying every skill and intuition I possess to planning all my negotiations. There are better ways to go than mindlessly starting negotiations and letting things play out to see what happens. That approach only works if you're lucky and negotiating with an amateur. Plan ahead no matter how much money is on the line.

What differentiates every negotiation I've done is the people on the other side of the table. The subject matter is always secondary and is almost irrelevant to how the negotiation will go and how successful I might be. I've negotiated everything from satellites and jet fighters to furniture and television sets. The process, strategy, and fundamental principles I've employed for these items have remained the same. I adapt and modify the specialized tactics to persuade the individual I'm dealing with.

For example, I won't negotiate with a corporate chief executive officer (CEO) in the same way as a furniture store owner. I'm also not going to negotiate with a CEO in the same way as a kidnapper, terrorist, or hostage-taker. These people have individual backgrounds, motivations, and thought processes that I intend to use to my advantage whenever possible. Simply put, they consistently think and act differently in response to whatever I might say or do.

A store owner depends on daily sales to pay his mortgage and put food on the table. He's likely an expert in his business and has a major stake in its success. Every dollar I take from him in a negotiation is one less dollar he has to spend on himself and his family. Conversely, the CEO is independent of a particular negotiation to fund his lifestyle. He's probably not a negotiation expert, but he likely has employees working for him who are.

The CEO's motivation is far less personal than the store owner's, and he won't go hungry if I take money from his company in a negotiation. He knows that, I know that, and I'll use tactics that take advantage of his executive status as someone who has less to lose if I snare an extra chunk of money when we shake hands on a deal.

Investigate the negotiation history of the person you'll be dealing with. Understanding their established patterns and strategies enables you to counteract them more effectively. Does this person have significant negotiating experience? If so, learn as much as possible about their operating mode. One way to do this is to talk to business associates who have worked for or with that person professionally. Experienced negotiators have a track record that could contain valuable information, and many develop patterns and certain styles you can use to your advantage.

If the other party tends to use the same tactics repeatedly, develop a plan that leverages your strengths while capitalizing on their weaknesses. Ascertain relevant information about the other party that will most benefit you. This process may not be feasible if you're in a retail business with a continuous inflow of new customers. Do some advance homework to determine if the other party operates under constraints that improve your relative position. You can use that information to your advantage if they're under pressure to hit sales targets or live within a tight budget.

If you're buying a product or service, do enough research to become reasonably familiar with the subject of the negotiation. The seller is at a distinct advantage if they detect you lack a basic understanding of the details, making you a prime target for a bluff or other techniques designed to instill anxiety and uncertainty. The more astute you are at the outset, the more sway you can exercise as you engage in detailed discussions.

Assume I want to buy two oil paintings by contemporary artists for my home. I don't have to be an expert in that field to start shopping, but if I'm unaware of what art is currently selling for, how can I make an intelligent offer? The asking price for art is rarely the final price paid. Since every oil painting is unique, there's no conceivable way to assess value definitively. Agreeing to the asking price is a gift to the seller because most will expect you to negotiate. If you don't, you're paying too much.

Research a few artists you're interested in and look at recent sales to establish a price range. This was difficult to do before the internet, but now anyone can dig up information previously accessible only to dealers and appraisers. If you're looking for expensive art for investment and enjoyment, consider hiring the services of an expert to assist you. Otherwise, you may make a bad deal that you'll soon regret.

Before starting the negotiation, define your success criteria and primary goal. It may or may not be the best price. For example, if you're building a new home and must move in before the first snow-fall, the completion schedule may be your paramount objective. You want to ensure the contractor will meet milestones and keep his promises. One way to do that is to couple interim performance milestones with financial incentives to motivate the contractor to work as efficiently and quickly as possible. He'll make more or less money, depending on whether he's ahead or behind schedule.

I usually have a price target before I start negotiations that's not cast in stone. It's based on realistic expectations considering all the constraints that will undoubtedly surface. If it's not a private negotiation, these may include budget limits, direction from man-agement, pressure to make sales targets, and other external forces. If it's a personal matter, it usually comes down to whether or not you can afford the item and how badly you want it.

I live by two rules: (1) Ask for what you want, not what you think you can get, and (2) You'll never get it for less than your first offer. People routinely violate these rules and then wonder why they end up with a bad deal. It's a common mistake when making offers on real estate.

Even when the asking price is far too high, buyers are reluctant to make a lowball offer, fearing they won't be taken seriously or they'll offend the seller. They should have the opposite fear; they'll overpay and kick themselves after doing it.

Your aggressiveness will depend on market conditions, primarily supply and demand. If you go to an auction and are the only bidder on an antique lantern, you'll probably own it for a very attractive price. But if the five people bidding against you all know it's a rare piece, there's an excellent chance you'll pay top dollar to own it. When the gavel drops, that's a good indication of fair market value on that day.

Resist the temptation to chase a rising market driven by fiscal stimulus and inflationary pressures. I appreciate the difficulty in waiting for more favorable buying conditions when you've watched prices climb for several years. You begin to feel the upward momentum will never stop, and you'll be priced out of the market forever.

This feeling is symptomatic of a psychological principle that's part of human nature. On average, we're influenced more by trends and the direction of things than what we see in a static snapshot in time. So, although the economy may appear robust on the surface, people should be focused on the storm clouds that portend trouble and weakness ahead. This explains why deflation can be so dangerous over the long term. If you expect asset prices to fall over the next few years, why would you consider buying now rather than later?

One certainty about negotiations is there will be no shortage of surprises. They become more predictable once you've gone through the wringer several times and gotten burned by your tactical errors. They'll most likely occur near the end, where they'll invariably inflict the most punishment. For example, you're about to close the deal, and the other party informs you of a delay in projected delivery dates. Do you incorporate that news into your price negotiation or look for another supplier? If your schedule is tight, you may have little choice.

Use the information you collect during the negotiation and stay alert for troubling warning signs. When the other party throws a wrench into a relatively smooth process up to that point, stop what you're doing and don't react immediately. Take the time to assess what it does to your plan and reevaluate it for possible workarounds. You've invested substantial time in this process and want to preserve your achievements. In the final analysis, make them pay for unanticipated changes that directly and indirectly force you to alter your plan.

What's It Worth?

Something is worth what someone else is willing and able to pay for it. While we may think we own something of sizable monetary value, we'll only know its actual worth if we sell it. Until then, we can only estimate the value of any item. There are several ways available to make that estimate an educated one.

There's no better way to determine the market value for an item than a public auction. A live auction provides real-time information on the values of all the items sold that day. Once the bidding starts, what you think it's worth becomes irrelevant. Multiple bidders competing for the same item will push up the price until the bidding stops and the auctioneer declares the item "sold." When he raps his gavel at the final bid, it's hard to argue the item is worth more or less. It sold for what someone else thought it was worth, period. We can all debate whether he paid too little or too much, but until it sells again, the bidders have established fair market values for that and similar items.

Flea markets and yard sales also provide a pretty good idea of worth, but the asking price is not necessarily the eventual sale price. I view the sticker price as the starting price and always intend to pay less than that. The only exceptions I'll make to that rule of thumb are small-dollar items the owner does not overvalue. It's not worth it to bicker over a few dollars. Choose your battles and save the hardball negotiating for when it matters.

Professional appraisals are a popular method to establish value, especially in real estate. Most banks will only approve a mortgage loan if a property appraisal is sufficiently high to justify the loan amount. If you're interested in purchasing a specific house, consider getting an appraisal before making an offer. The risk is that your appraisal will be higher than the asking price. The seller would likely discover that fact because a proper appraisal would require a thorough inspection of the house, including the interior. That could only happen with the seller's permission. As a potential buyer, I steer clear of appraisals because I want the freedom to negotiate without artificial boundaries. The seller may have limits, but I'll deal with those as the negotiation progresses.

Other than actual sale prices, everything else is someone's estimated value. An estimate is only as good as the estimator, and no estimator is perfect. I guarantee you'd get ten different results if you hired ten appraisers to appraise the same house. That's reality, but if you hire three appraisers and they're all within 10% of each other, that's a reasonably good indicator of market value.

Exercise caution when hiring an appraiser who's an expert in the specific fields you're interested in. If you want to know what a piece of old furniture is worth, find someone well-versed in the field of antiques. Ask for credentials and references from appraisers to assess their qualifications for your particular needs. There are national appraisal associations, such as the American Society of Appraisers, that can help you find one with the expertise you're seeking.

It's common for at least one of the parties in a negotiation to work with an estimated value they obtained via one of the valuation methods discussed. At their discretion, they may disclose how they arrived at their offer or counteroffer. If they have an appraisal that works in their favor, they'll likely share it and may even provide you with a copy. This disclosure makes for a tougher negotiation since they'll use that as leverage to justify whatever position they adopt. In such cases, consider paying for an appraisal completed by someone you trust. The danger is that this devolves into a battle of dueling appraisals, much like a court trial that devolves into a battle of dueling experts that usually does more to confuse the jury than help it make a reasoned decision.

When the other party uses an appraisal to bolster their position, I outwardly ignore it. An appraisal is one person's opinion of what something is worth. I don't have to agree with it, and I'll use as many facts as possible to dismantle the assumptions and calculations that form the basis for their position. I'd much rather shoot holes in their appraisal than stand on one I commissioned.

I recently had an experience that sheds light on how I've dealt with cost proposals from home improvement contractors. Upgrades and remodels can be intimidating if you know little about construction. When you see how much the job will cost, how do you determine if it's fair and reasonable?

When I purchased my house in 2012, the exterior consisted of T1-11 siding that had been stained rather than painted. It's an economical and convenient choice for those seeking a natural, woodgrain appearance with a rustic aesthetic. I quickly found out how much red-bellied woodpeckers love it. It was a nonstop battle to keep them from attacking the house, and one that I consistently lost. Part of the problem was the gray stain made the T1-11 resemble the bark of a tree with a similar texture. The birds concluded it was close enough for their purposes, and my house became a nesting place for every woodpecker in the neighborhood.

After several years, it became apparent that I had to replace and repaint some of my trim and fascia boards. The entire house needed to be restained or painted, something I expected to do at some point when I bought it. There was also the issue of what to do about the woodpecker holes that were scattered throughout.

The solution I decided on was vinyl siding because it simultaneously solved all the problems I had to deal with. First, the siding could go right over the T1-11 without doing anything to it. Second, in the areas where the T1-11 was damaged, it could be replaced by regular plywood. Third, the vinyl trim would cover and protect all the trim boards, with only a few needing replacements. Fourth, the new siding would increase the resale value of my house and avoid a considerable amount of future maintenance.

I assembled a list of what I wanted done and asked for a quote from a local contractor. He came over, took photos, and walked the property while taking notes. I received his proposal about a week later, considerably exceeding my expected price. His number was so high that I felt it would be unproductive to waste my time (or his) negotiating with him. I had a couple of other contractors in mind, so I sent one of them my list. He did an inspection and sent me his proposal. It was within a few percent of the first one, and I was shocked again.

Any plans I had to leverage one proposal against the other vanished immediately. In a sense, I had two different "appraisals" with essentially the same answer. I know people who'd assume that because the two proposals were so close, they must be in the ballpark of the project's ultimate cost. It's understandable, but my gut told me something was wrong, and I had to figure out what it was. I had to go on the offensive and decided to use a tactic I call the "Trap Door."

Before going to trial, lawyers know the answers to the questions they plan to ask in the courtroom. They obtain most of those answers by deposing key witnesses and performing document discovery. To resolve the enormous disconnect in the proposals I'd received, I enlisted the assistance of my brother, who has tons of experience in general contracting. His field audit yielded a measurement of 2,385 square feet, establishing the baseline amount of siding required to cover the entire house and garage. I'd set the trap and wouldn't divulge that number to contractors until after I saw their numbers. I already knew the answer to the question I would ask them.

I contacted the second contractor, whose bid was slightly lower, and asked him how many square feet of siding were included in his total cost estimate and how he calculated the number. The answer was 4,670 square feet and was computed by a surface area algorithm based on aerial photographs of my house. I knew roofing contractors frequently used aerial surveys to produce estimates, but I didn't realize such surveys were used for siding estimates. I knew why his 4,670 square footage was almost double my brother's 2,385.

My house appears to be one story when viewed from the street, but it's built into the side of a hill. A walk around the back reveals two stories, with the first floor only exposed along the back wall. The rest of the first floor is below ground level. Therefore, siding was required for the entire second floor and only the back wall of the first floor. I asked the contractor if he'd send me the full report from the vendor that did the analysis. I received the report and reviewed all the photos and schematics with associated measurements.

The report revealed numerous discrepancies that overstated the measured area. The giveaway was the schematic showing elevations of each section of the house. I have a one-story garage, and the schematic showed a front wall height of 15 feet. The wall is actually eight feet with a sloped roof that peaks at about 15 feet. So, the survey was based on installing siding from ground level to the roof's peak, roughly equivalent to a two-story garage. The entire house had similar problems, so it's no wonder his numbers were grossly inflated. As a result, I sent this note to the contractor.

I have a theory about the [siding estimate] report. As I mentioned previously, two things made it difficult to measure my house from the air: (1) Much of it is obscured by trees, and (2) It's built into the side of a hill. Looking at the photos they included, the only clear aerial view with the best sight-angle is the back of the house and about half of the garage. That would lead one to conclude this is a two-story house all the way around when, in fact, much of the first story obscured in the photos is below ground. Their computer model calculated elevations based on a normal above-ground, two-story house, including a two-story garage, which would account for their exaggerated square footage estimates. They didn't have the photos or data necessary to correct this, which is an obvious limitation to their aerial-only estimation process.

Bingo. I knew the rough dimensions of my house, so I ran some numbers based on the report's square footage, then deducted three sides of the first floor that would not be sided. I calculated the total could be at most 2,500 square feet compared to the contractor's estimate of 4,670. My rough calculation of 2,500 based on my adjustments to the report solidified my confidence in my brother's field measurement of 2,385.

I didn't pass on either of my numbers to the contractor because I expected him to do an on-site measurement due to my note, and I wanted it to be completely independent of what my brother and I had done. Not surprisingly, his revised estimate came in at 2,400, and down the trap door he plummeted. In a heartbeat, his proposal had been obliterated. This is an example of how to create leverage that you can exploit at any point in the negotiation to reduce the price or add scope to the job at no additional cost. I agreed to base our contract on his 2,400-square-foot estimate. Ultimately, he still got his number, and I got what I wanted to slash the cost. I let him find his way to the correct answer.

The work was completed to my satisfaction, and both parties walked away happy. This result is often referred to as a "win-win" negotiation because it exemplifies the outcome where both sides get what they want. I'd rather win outright than lose, but I'll settle for a win-win when it's clearly my most viable option. As a bonus, there's significant value in finding experienced contractors who do quality work at a fair price. I now had someone I could call on for future projects.

While we eventually arrived at a mutually agreeable price, I recognized that I'd thrown his entire estimating system into disarray.

I had no idea how long he'd relied on aerial surveys for his siding proposals, and I never asked. It's his business and his decision on how he approaches subsequent jobs like mine. I hope he improved his estimating process to avoid pricing errors that might impact future customers.

The good news is that my house looks great with the vinyl siding, and the contractor made a fair profit for his labor. However, this isn't always possible in the real world because "fairness" is a highly subjective term open to interpretation. Regardless of the outcome's circumstances, I'm determined to prevail in every negotiation based on my personal goals. If the other party considers it a win for their side, too, that's even better.

There are critical lessons to be learned from this experience. I've identified them sequentially as distinct points but listed them in no particular order. Their relative importance will vary as a function of the unique parameters of each negotiation.

First, start negotiations only when you're ready. In this case, I received two proposals that my instincts told me were far too high. If I had chosen either proposal to negotiate a contract, arriving at an agreeable number would have been tough because their square footage numbers were almost twice as large as mine. How could we close that gap without being completely arbitrary?

In my former line of work, the first step in evaluating all proposals was to perform a "sanity test." It wasn't complicated and required minimal analysis. We looked at the proposed number, and based on our collective knowledge and experience, we determined if it was inside or outside the ballpark of what we expected. If it was inside, we started negotiations. If it was outside, we asked the bidder to reevaluate their proposal to ensure it complied with our statement of work and specifications. Often, they discovered an error that was overlooked during their review process. If my siding contractor had done this when he received the square footage estimate from his vendor, he could have corrected it before I saw it.

Second, if you can blow up a proposal and destroy the rationale supporting it, do it. In my example, put yourself in the other party's position. You just got your head handed to you and were exposed as a contractor who wildly overbid a routine job. I'm confident this was not intentional. The contractor hired a company to generate the measurement report and relied on it, as I'm sure he'd done many times before. An experienced contractor who walked my property should have recognized that the provided number was too high. It's evident to anyone who sees my house that three-quarters of the first floor is buried in dirt and isn't going to require siding.

A mistake such as this immediately puts the other party on the defensive, exactly where you want them to be. You gain substantial leverage that remains after the error is corrected. The contractor knew he couldn't afford to make another mistake and cause further damage to his credibility. When a contractor makes an unforced error like this, he's less likely to be aggressive during negotiations. Unfortunate oversights have a way of tamping down aggressive actions and reactions by the other party. There's nothing unethical about using the resulting leverage to your advantage. Always remember the other party will use whatever leverage they can gain against you.

Third, never take anything at face value. Nothing is exempt from being analyzed and questioned. Do not be shy and accommodating. Your money is on the line, and you're the only one who can and will protect it.

Before signing a contract for goods or services, always read the fine print, be bold, and challenge the boilerplate language. Companies use boilerplate for many reasons, but the unmistakable one is purely psychological. When such a contract is placed in front of you, all professionally typed and structured, it projects an air of invincibility, authenticity, and intimidation. If you dare to challenge the status quo, you're made to feel that you don't understand what you're doing or who you're dealing with. You're just supposed to accept it and move on.

Sometimes, you have no choice. Classic examples are the agreements that accompany free computer software downloads. To start the process, you must "Agree" or "Accept" every term and condition, or the download button won't work. Most agreements are so detailed and complicated that I'd be shocked if even 1% of those wanting the software read the entire thing. They assume there's nothing in there to worry about. One can only hope.

These downloads define the take-it-or-leave-it proposition because the software company has all the leverage. They're giving away the software! They have no incentive to waste their time negotiating with you. Do you want the software? Hit the button! If not, goodbye and good luck!

This approach is powerful and effective. When was the last time you questioned a loan document you were asked to sign? How about a purchase agreement to buy a car? A ton of fine print buried there could come back to bite you if the deal sours for any reason.

Either I sign this contract, or I won't get what I want. That might be true, but more often than not, it isn't. The only way you'll find out is by voicing your reservations and making it clear that the document as currently constituted is unacceptable.

As a first-time book author, I discovered that no two publishers are alike. I also learned they have significant leverage because the supply of unsolicited manuscripts exceeds the demand for new books. As the volume of book proposals exploded along with the advent of e-books, the publishing landscape changed dramatically. Most books are now entirely or partially self-published, meaning the author fronts some or all of the cost to get the book to market. Traditional publishers can be very picky about who gets a book deal and who doesn't, and some of their boilerplate contracts contain language that grants them nearly plenary power over the author.

Before I decided to independently self-publish my book, I received a proposal from a publisher that contained the following key elements.

- My upfront cost: $8,800. The publisher offered four tiers of publishing packages, providing the author with basic through premier levels of services. The option at this price point is the one I was considering.

- The publisher retained unilateral authority to modify the contract at any time and for any reason. If the author objected to any changes, their only option was to terminate the agreement.

What's the point of signing an agreement if the other party can take your money and change it without your consent? There were other oppressive provisions I didn't like, especially the paltry royalty percentages, but I decided to submit a counteroffer that accepted some of the less burdensome ones. The clause I couldn't accept was the unilateral modification authority that the publisher could use to blow up the agreement.

The response to my counteroffer was that the boilerplate contract was take-it-or-leave-it, so I left it. When negotiation is not an option, your decision-making process becomes simple. You either accept the dictate, or you don't.

Fortunately, it didn't take long to ascertain that my best option was to take control of the process and contract out what I couldn't do myself. This book is the result. I wrote and edited 100% of the text and designed the front and back covers. It's all on me, so it sinks or swims on my watch.

One of the biggest mistakes I've observed is that people assume things to be true without ever testing them. My rule is to presume nothing, especially when your instincts and common sense steer you off the proverbial path. At the end of the path is a trap designed to steal any leverage you started with.

This discussion isn't about trust. I'm not saying or implying that the people you choose to do business with can't be trusted. Never assume that those on the other side of the negotiating table are knocking themselves out to further your best interests. They're in business to make money, so their best interests are paramount, as they should be. However, that doesn't mean they're lying, deceiving, mistreating, or taking advantage of you. They're entitled to a fair profit, but you get to vote on what that will be.

The vast majority of contractors, small business owners, and others I've negotiated with have been hardworking, trustworthy people with whom I wouldn't hesitate to do business again. For some, I've had references who attested to their credibility and integrity, but they all had to earn my trust. Even though they may be treating you honestly, mistakes happen. If you believe there's too much margin in the price they're quoting, it's up to you to remove it. If they're going to take your money, you have the right to probe, ask questions, and do whatever it takes to ensure fair and equitable treatment. I faithfully adhere to my fundamental negotiating principles regardless of who they are.

The art of negotiating represents business in its purest form, so keep the other party at arm's length as you work your way through the process. Your attitude toward them can evolve as you gain more experience working with them. If you hire a contractor who does superior work for you at a fair price, you'll likely hire him again. That second negotiation will look considerably different from the first because a level of integrity and confidence has been established that may not have existed the first time around.

Fourth, look for the obvious, and don't be excessively detail-oriented at the beginning of a negotiation. Resist the initial impulse to do a bottom-up analysis of a price proposal and scrutinize every nickel and dime. There's a time for that, but it's later rather than sooner. Look at the bottom line and ask yourself if it makes sense. If you're installing a new deck on your house and a contractor submits a bid twice what you expected, a flashing red light alerts you there's a problem. You don't need a detailed analysis to reach that conclusion.

In the siding example, I had two contractors submit similar bids. The similarity presents a form of confirmation bias that tempts you to assume that since they're so close, each bid affirms the reasonableness of the other. As demonstrated by my example, that's a dangerous assumption because both contractors were wildly off with their estimates. Using the same vendor to provide the square footage calculations for my house would explain the closeness of their bids. Even if they didn't, the odds are that both used estimates derived from aerial surveys performed by different sources using similar algorithms. It's much easier to do it from the air and presumably cheaper than paying someone to take manual measurements, especially on a two-story house. The contractor can also shift some of the responsibility for inaccuracies to the company preparing the survey.

Remember that a price quotation is just a number regardless of what it's for. You can choose to accept it, reject it, laugh at it, or ignore it. When two contractors get it wrong, you're on notice that critical analysis of whatever they give you is crucial. An estimate presented to you as a take-it-or-leave-it proposition should be thoroughly scrutinized before responding. My knee-jerk reaction is to reject it, but I'll consider it if it's something I really want or can't do without. As tempted as I might be to accept it, I assume it's negotiable until proven otherwise. Even if something is advertised as nonnegotiable, I'll make a counteroffer because I have nothing to lose.

Unfortunately, many assume prices are only negotiable in the U.S. when buying a big-ticket item like a house or car. Much of this is cultural and a function of our upbringing. The vast majority of buying and selling happens in a retail format. You walk into a store, and there's a price tag that identifies the asking price. Almost without exception, people take their items to the checkout counter and pay those prices without question. Online shopping is even more restrictive because if you want to negotiate the price, there's no one there to deal with. Dealing via email or chat doesn't work well because the person at the other end of the conversation usually lacks the authority to adjust prices.

Why are Americans locked in to paying sticker price most of the time? It's the norm and how it's been done in the past. It's how your parents did it. It's accepted. I'm telling you to throw that thinking out the window. You don't have to accept it, and nothing prevents you from negotiating whenever and wherever you want. The other party may not consent to negotiating, but you'll only know that's the case if you try. Until you get a refusal, press on as though everything is negotiable.

Negotiation is all about assessing and establishing value without the benefit of an auction or competitive marketplace. You have a position, and the other party has a position. It's important to understand that neither position may be based on science, mathematics, economics, facts, or fairness. The numbers are often arbitrary and based on wishful thinking or a back-of-the-envelope calculation.

A prime example of this is a civil lawsuit for defamation. It's virtually impossible to accurately calculate future damages stemming from defamation. You can claim lost employment opportunities and wages, lower wages, lost friendships, and many other things that may or may not ever happen. The celebrity factor of being sued creates free publicity that might benefit you in the long run. The plaintiffs fabricate damage amounts, even when supposedly backed up by detailed analysis. We used to call this a WAG, or wild-ass guess. If we had any rational basis for the guess, however small it might be, we called it a SWAG, or scientific wild-ass guess. The numbers are always intentionally high for one reason: When settlement negotiations commence, you've got plenty of money to give away to get a deal.

The question of value always arises in financial investing, whether it be stocks, bonds, mutual funds, cryptocurrencies, or any other financial asset. Investors use several methods to gauge value and decide to buy and sell assets. There's one in particular I'll focus on because I've witnessed it in play many times. Whenever I mention it, it generates instant conflict and controversy. It's called The Greater Fool Theory (GFT) and can be applied to any asset class.

GFT suggests you buy an asset whose price is rising simply because there will be a greater fool (than you) in the future who will pay more for it than you did. The theory is that even if the asset is already overvalued relative to standard measures and has little to no intrinsic value, you should still invest in it if there are sufficient greater fools out there to keep pushing prices higher. If the supply of greater fools were unlimited, so the theory goes, everyone would make money along the way until the end of time.

The earliest documented example of this I'm aware of is the Great Dutch Tulip Bubble of 1637. Tulip bulbs were introduced to Holland in 1593, and the price bubble took off in earnest in 1634. As prices began to rise, more people started buying bulbs, often relying on credit. This buying frenzy fueled speculation and irrational expectations as the craze spread throughout the country. Massive price spikes created a positive feedback cycle, and people became convinced that exponential price inflation was here to stay. Unfortunately, the never-ending supply of greater fools and their money eventually vanished, and prices collapsed. Investors finally realized what they should have known from the beginning; that irrational price inflation was unsustainable and would eventually cause a massive selloff. Many of them went bankrupt as a result.

At the height of the bubble, it's estimated that one premium tulip bulb commanded the same price as a mansion on the Amsterdam Grand Canal. How is that even possible? I witnessed the same foolish buying hysteria during the dot-com stock bubble that peaked in March 2000. When it finally bottomed in October 2002, the Nasdaq Composite stock market index had lost 78% of its value.

I had a front-row seat to the psychology behind the massive bubble in technology stocks, particularly those in the internet sector. I vividly remember getting a call from a friend in early

1999 who recommended I buy stock in Yahoo. I was familiar with its search engine but knew little about the company or its primary income sources. I asked my friend how the company made money, and he didn't know either. When I asked why he bought the stock, he answered, "Because it's going up." This is a classic example of the GFT in action. He was swept up in the hysteria and assumed there would always be greater fools prepared to pay a higher price than he did.

Unfortunately for my friend, he never sold the stock and held it as it crashed, forever believing it would make a comeback. It never did. The lesson learned is that it's hazardous to value an asset based solely on what you think the next guy will pay for it. If that asset doesn't have some underlying intrinsic value tied to actual demand and is not a buying fad or frenzy, be very cautious and do your homework and due diligence. Prices can plunge faster than they went up when the momentum fades and the panicked herd heads for the exits, leaving you holding the bag.

Are we witnessing the GFT in action again with the advent of cryptocurrencies and nonfungible tokens (NFT)? There are vast differences of opinion on this, and the story is still unfolding. One notable NFT sale was the first tweet from Twitter cofounder Jack Dorsey, which brought in $2.9 million. About a year later, the new owner decided to sell it and pledged 50% of the proceeds to charity. He posted the listing with an opening bid of $48 million, believing someone would pay far more for it than he did. That's a prime example of the Greater Fool Theory on steroids. The highest reported bid I could find was $12,600, representing less than 0.5% of what he paid and 0.03% of his opening bid.

Another phenomenon that induces people to pay more for something than they otherwise would is the "fear of missing out." FOMO often accompanies GFT and can amplify its effects. It typically manifests when people see the value of an asset rising and believe if they don't buy it now, they'll miss out on all the future gains that await them. In addition, they won't be able to afford it as prices continue to rise.

We saw this develop with the escalation of housing prices during the COVID-19 pandemic as historically low interest rates and a surging money supply combined to drive prices skyward in a relatively short timeframe. The assumption that interest rates would likely rise over time provided further stimulation to buy now rather than later. Buyers were determined to enter the real estate market before being priced out completely. Bidding wars erupted in many areas, and people routinely paid significantly more than the asking price. Anyone attempting to negotiate the price down was not considered a serious buyer, so you either played the game or exited the market entirely. Buyers had little to no leverage, and the sellers knew it.

To the extent possible, I avoid negotiating when the other party has all or most of the leverage. I won't pay more for something based on fear or the assumption there will always be a greater fool who will pay even more than I did. Emotion can be your worst enemy if you let it influence or control how you spend your money.

Negotiations are more challenging when buying or selling certain assets and commodities. Examples are real estate, automobiles, antiques, artwork, and collectible coins and stamps. Their price movements are regularly tracked around the country and reported in various formats. If you're in the market for a used car, you'll have a tough time negotiating a price significantly different than what's quoted in the *Kelley Blue Book* (KBB). Whether you like it or not, many buyers and sellers treat it as the bible of car valuations. Similar books are available for coins, stamps, and other collectible items.

I want to share my views regarding the *Kelley Blue Book*. They're strictly my opinions, and I have no evidence to substantiate them. I'll boil it down to one question: Does KBB report prices or set prices? I believe, to a large extent, it sets prices. Let me explain.

Its website states, "The *Kelley Blue Book* Price Advisor shows you what you should pay for a new or used car based on what others have paid in your area." Ask yourself this question: To what extent does its pricing guide become a self-fulfilling prophecy? Car prices are dynamic and can change daily, and it's virtually impossible for KBB to continuously survey and update actual sales around the country to maintain an accurate database. What happens is that people refer to KBB and then pay that price or something close to it. Each sale validates the KBB price the buyer relied on and becomes a data point for the following survey. KBB is widely and frequently used as a source, so it's difficult to imagine prices deviating significantly from their published guidelines. The more people base their buying and selling decisions on it, the more it reaffirms itself as an accurate measure of what's happening in the marketplace.

I'd make the same observation about all such pricing guides, regardless of the subject matter. They all tend to become self-fulfilling prophecies once they're widely accepted as established, credible sources for pricing information. It reminds me of the old riddle about the chicken or the egg and which came first. While scientists have debated this question for years, it doesn't matter in the context of life as we know it today. However, when it comes to pricing guides, it definitely matters if the guides set prices rather than report them, even if accidental or unintentional. Relying on such guides is your choice, but I encourage you to distance yourself from them whenever advantageous to your position.

Several years ago, I bought a used car in a private sale. The seller told me the asking price was based on KBB, and they weren't inclined to take any less. The owner certainly has the right to assign whatever price they want, knowing that reliance on KBB gives them leverage that can be difficult to overcome.

In addition to objective criteria such as manufacturer, year, model, style, options, and mileage, KBB also asks you to rate the vehicle's overall condition as fair, good, very good, or excellent.

The owner is motivated to rate the car as highly as possible, but a subjective rating is open to challenge by the buyer. Before I made an offer, I did a KBB analysis based on the objective inputs and my evaluation of the car's condition. The KBB valuation model yielded an estimate lower than the asking price. I assume it resulted from a difference in our subjective ratings, which provided me sufficient maneuvering room to structure a counteroffer. We eventually settled around 9% less than the asking price. That wasn't a noteworthy reduction, but it was better than zero.

When confronted by a pricing guide such as KBB, don't allow yourself to be pressured into accepting it. They're guides and no more than that. I refuse to be constrained by any guide that may have the unintended effect of setting prices. A negotiation is not a court of law, and there are no rules of evidence. I don't have to prove my opinions to anyone, and I certainly have the right to say what I believe. By the same token, the person using the guide is not obligated to agree with me, and that's precisely the point. We're negotiating because we disagree and are trying to resolve our differences to reach an agreement. We'll only get there if each side is willing to make concessions regardless of their preconceived notions of value.

Today's technology provides a variety of ways to research market values independently. Many of these resources are free and can be easily accessed online. I prefer to select and compare a diversity of sources rather than rely on just one or two. This approach helps eliminate bias and provides a more representative sample of data to inform you about what's happening in the marketplace.

The eBay platform is one example of a giant open market where you can find an array of pricing information for all kinds of things. Many websites specialize in real estate, automobiles, motorcycles, boats, airplanes, cameras, watches, collectibles, and other items covered in detail. Popular websites for housing include Zillow, Trulia, and Realtor. Again, be careful to distinguish between asking prices and sale prices since negotiators rarely pay the asking price. Whenever possible, I rely on prices at which goods are currently changing hands between buyers and sellers.

Libraries carry an assortment of sources such as *Consumer Reports*, *Kelley Blue Book*, and many others. If people collect something, chances are there has been at least one book written about it, many with pricing guides. No matter what method you choose to determine value, they all represent estimates of varying reliability. For items of potentially significant value, use multiple techniques and then compare them. If they yield similar results, you're in the ballpark of approximate value. If you're uncomfortable with the results, dig deeper and expand your research.

Find a kink in the armor of the other party and discover where they're vulnerable. Use that as an entry point to go after bigger targets later on. When you're up against someone using a pricing guide as their anchor position, remember there's no requirement that you even consider it, much less use it as a trusted source. It's you against them, so use every tool in your arsenal to promote your position over theirs.

The Scarcity Effect

The scarcity effect is a simple concept based on how the average person values something that doesn't have a price already attached to it. The less available a product is, the more they will appreciate it now because they question its future availability and the possibility of an escalating price. It's another way of expressing the economic principle of "supply and demand," but with less emphasis on the demand component.

Buyers' behavior can also be impacted unexpectedly, defying basic economics. Under the right conditions, people will perceive higher values even when the supply is not limited. There are psychological aspects to this that have been explored and researched by marketing professionals to maximize sales and profits through targeted advertising. It's a form of leverage often used in short-term marketing campaigns that may have a limited shelf life once the restricted supply perception wears off.

A vital aspect of perceived scarcity is popularity. The logical assumption is that if a product is highly popular, its price is supported by that demand and is subject to going higher. Apple has successfully used this strategy in marketing the iPhone by creating the impression that supplies may be limited to bolster prices. History and Apple's consistent profitability tell us this approach has worked well over the years. Many iPhone fanatics are reluctant to assume the risk of what they perceive to be a potential lost opportunity. Interestingly, Apple has rarely failed to meet demand for its products over the near term.

Exclusivity and rarity similarly affect pricing but can be far more potent than popularity. Exclusive branding drives luxury companies such as Cartier, Rolex, Rolls-Royce, Gucci, Tiffany, Hermès, and Ferrari. Those companies enjoy the advantage of setting prices based on their reputations for selling high-end products to people who can afford them. They amplify this effect by offering small production runs of limited-edition products only available to those willing to pay the list price. By restricting the time these products are available, they pressure customers to yield to those established prices.

Another way they make customers feel special is by creating a sense of urgency around new product offerings and discontinued items. If you want them, you best mount your horse, find the nearest retailer, and swipe that credit card before you miss out. People have an inherent fear of losing out. It's absolutely palpable. Watch videos of Black Friday shoppers in any large retailer, and you'll see people climbing over each other to scoop up the last laptop on fire sale.

As a fourth-class cadet at USAFA, I invested in a watch that would withstand the rigors of the academy regimen. The one I wanted was available in the cadet store for $125, brand new in the box. James Bond fans will recognize it as a later model of the stainless steel watch Sean Connery wore in 1962's *Dr. No*. I'll never forget the store clerk's reaction when I told her I wanted to buy the Rolex Submariner: "I can't imagine anyone paying that much for a watch." There was no negotiation since prices in the c-store were already rock-bottom, and cadets knew better than to try and cut them further. The c-store no longer sells Rolex watches because the company reduced the number of retailers to amplify their exclusivity. Submariner enthusiasts would immediately recognize mine as a reference number 1680 with the red "SUBMARINER" lettering on its face.

The impact of the Bond franchise on Rolex is immense. The company also formed alliances with famous explorers and athletes that elevated the brand when this type of marketing was far less prevalent than it is today. My watch has been everywhere with me: scuba diving, mountain climbing, survival training, weightless training, alpine skiing, airborne school, as well as a myriad of other adventures that put it to the test. It passed all of them with flying colors, and I still wear it to this day.

I got a wake-up call on price when I visited a local dealer to adjust a new bracelet I had purchased. The original one had finally given way to various forms of punishment I'd inflicted over the decades. I asked Rolex if I could buy the unique tool needed to adjust the bracelet to my wrist, but I discovered they don't sell them to the public. The good news was that authorized dealers perform the adjustment at no cost.

Exclusivity is just one of the ways that Rolex maintains its blue-chip reputation. When I bought the new bracelet directly from Rolex Watch USA in New York City, I discovered I had to exchange my original one to close the deal. This policy prevents that bracelet from showing up for sale online, which might dilute the authenticity of official Rolex products. Authorized dealers now exercise complete control over sales and distribution, which has propelled prices skyward. One benefit is the reduction of fake replica watches, although it's still a serious problem in some countries. While my original bracelet was authentic, its destruction prevented its resale. The policy also helps to boost prices because Rolex is the only source for genuine watches.

While at the dealer, I inquired about the price and availability of the current stainless Submariner. The quoted price was approximately 70 times what I paid for mine, and that was the good news. They had no Submariners in stock, weren't sure when it would be in stock, but hoped to receive one or two in the next six months. In addition, there was a long waitlist of buyers competing for whatever came in the door. To get around this, you could contact out-of-state dealers and offer to pay more than the asking price. Once again, this keeps prices elevated with no signs of coming down. I also know from experience that the cost to clean and recondition my self-winding watch is far more than I paid to buy it. Times have certainly changed in the rarefied world of Rolex.

Negotiating for any luxury brand is challenging and, in some cases, impossible. It's especially true during good economic times when asset values are rising, and the government borrows and prints plenty of money to keep them artificially propped up. If there's no urgency to what you're buying, you'll have better luck negotiating deals. Sellers experiencing revenue declines may compensate by lowering prices. Even if they don't, you have better leverage to make an offer that undercuts their asking price.

If high demand for a product is genuine and not simply perceived, this increases prices. Failure to meet demand because of shortages will fuel the fire on prices. If the uniqueness of the product suppresses any viable competition from similar products, this presents an impetus for further price pressures. All of these factors combine to create a sense of urgency among some consumers who believe that buying now will get you the best deal, and if you don't buy, that product may no longer be available. This type of thinking is what sellers want you to believe, even if it's not true or not as bad as you think it is.

Overall, economic conditions play a prominent role in creating authentic and invalid scarcity of supply dynamics. For example, real estate prices react directly to anecdotal evidence of cash buyers making multiple offers above the asking price. A seller's market feeds on itself, driving prices even higher as the competition for a shrinking inventory intensifies. When mortgage rates are low and the money supply is at record levels, that's all the rocket fuel you need to push prices beyond the measurable affordability threshold.

The scarcity effect relies on the basic economics of supply and demand but is also heavily driven by consumer perception. High demand may cause people to think a product is scarce when it isn't.

Under normal economic conditions, if I go to a store and the beer I want is out of stock, that doesn't necessarily mean the product is scarce. Perhaps a customer recently bought 20 cases for a big party and cleaned out the store. Or it could be that I arrived at the store a few hours before their next beer delivery. Even though I perceive a product as being scarce, it could be a matter of bad timing. I shouldn't allow my misperception to alter the price I'll pay for the beer.

Retailers are known for playing head games to maximize sales and profits. There's nothing illegal or unethical about it, and you can't blame them if you fall for it. They want you to believe shopping with them is a take-it-or-leave-it proposition, which is why it's almost unheard of for them to offer to negotiate with you. The burden is almost always on you to take the initiative to make that happen.

The best way to protect yourself as a buyer is to determine the actual supply and demand for a product before you buy it. Sometimes, this may be challenging, but the internet is an effective research tool containing mountains of free information. Absent facts to the contrary, act as though supply and demand are not an issue until proven otherwise. This approach provides room to maneuver on price if you later discover evidence that they're an impactful factor.

The Twelve Fundamental Principles of Negotiation

1. Ask for what you want, not what you think you can get

There's a persistent fear that if you're too aggressive in a negotiation and appear to be taking advantage of the other party, this will antagonize and upset them to the point where no deal is possible. You're afraid you'll insult them, they'll think you're cheap, and they'll say you're the last person on the planet they'll do business with.

While those outcomes are possible, don't throw in the towel before entering the ring. Do a risk assessment considering several interconnected factors, including who you're dealing with, the relative leverage of both parties, and the overall complexity of the negotiation. If I have significantly more leverage than they do, I don't care who they are and how they react to my first offer.

If you judge negotiation success on getting only what you think is ultimately possible, you've effectively reduced the size of the prize before leaving the gate. Set the bar beyond what you believe is attainable and realistic because you always want to leave yourself room to negotiate. Always. What you think you can get may be where you end up, but it's not where you want to begin. Establish your objectives and design a strategy to achieve them.

While getting your price is usually a high priority, you may enter negotiations with a range of goals that will be your measure of success. Make a list of what you want, what you need, what you're willing to give up, and what you won't negotiate. The list may change as the process unfolds, but you'll be better positioned to evaluate those decisions if you start with a clear statement of your objectives and the basis for each. That clarity will help drive the negotiation to a conclusion.

When developing your objectives, use all your data, including any relevant research to determine price targets and potential negotiating tactics. The more you know at the beginning, the stronger your position will be as you trade offers.

Never assume the other party thinks like you do or that their perspective on what constitutes success mirrors yours. What you view as outrageous or outlandish may be perfectly reasonable to them. The only way you'll find out where they drew their line in the sand is to open negotiations at a price point that's guaranteed to generate a forceful reaction. You've set the bar too low if you don't strike a nerve. Don't agonize over offending the other party. If it happens, it happens, but you can't build your negotiation strategy around fear of the unknown.

Remember that as the negotiation progresses, your goal may change based on modifications in scope and other unforeseen actions by either party. However, these potential occurrences should not constrain your first offer or counteroffer. If you don't shoot for the stars, it will be much harder to get to the Moon.

2. You'll never get it for less than your first offer

If there's no asking price, is it better to make the first offer or let the other party do it? While there are strong opinions on both sides of this question, my answer is that it depends. More importantly, sometimes you have no choice. Most car dealerships mark their cars with an asking price. That's the first offer, and the ball is in your court to either accept it, make a counteroffer, or walk away. I don't like being in that position, so unless there's a good reason not to, I prefer to put the first number on the table.

Let's analyze the question from an alternate perspective. Assume there's a negotiation that lasts several months, and during that time, there are 25 offers and counteroffers before the parties finally settle. If I asked you to identify the most important offer of all, what would it be? It's tempting to say the last offer that both parties agreed to. Whatever methods they employed to get to the final number are no longer relevant. They resolved their differences, and it's over. Done. End of story.

My answer would be that the most important offer is the first offer, irrespective of which party made it. The first offer is the "anchor" price that becomes the baseline against which all subsequent offers will be compared and measured. Even if that price is considered unreasonable by the other party, they're stuck with it even if they reject it or make a counteroffer. If that offer is countered, it will be touted as a percentage increase to the anchor price, even though that percentage is irrelevant to the negotiation.

Attaching an enduring personal bias to whatever you see or hear first is human nature. You'll never forget it, no matter what happens after that. For example, most people remember their first kiss, but how many remember the fourth or fifth? That bias is influential in a negotiation context because it locks the brain into thinking that any deviation from the anchor must be explained or justified. The fact is that it doesn't, but getting around that predisposition can be challenging. The other party will want to know why your number is better than theirs, even though the original number may have no rational basis. This can force a psychological momentum shift because responding to the anchor can put you on defense when you'd much rather be on offense. Setting the anchor makes it much easier to dictate the future path of the negotiation.

If you're positioned to set the anchor, you have more leverage if you know more about the subject of the negotiation than the other party. Assume your neighbor has a nice boat you'd like to buy, but it's not currently for sale. Nothing stops you from making an offer, but you're at a significant disadvantage because he knows much more about his boat than you do.

Before floating a number, research the make and model and determine the estimated market value based on its current condition. Then, set the anchor below that value if you make an offer, but not so far below that your neighbor would quickly reject it. Remember, the boat isn't for sale, so you've got to make the offer attractive enough to get your neighbor to at least think about selling.

Set the anchor before the boat owner comes up with an asking price. Since he's not seriously considering selling the boat, he's likely to put a high price on it, figuring there's nothing to lose if there are no offers. The psychology works in his favor. The problem is that once he sets that anchor price, he's already established a bias that will be difficult to undo.

Be very aggressive when you know significantly more than the other party about the subject of the negotiation. If you're an art expert and attend an auction selling valuable oil paintings, it's reasonable to assume you know at least as much about art as any other bidders. When both parties are experts, the anchor will carry less weight since it will be discounted if considered unreasonable. Experts have a better appreciation of market value and are far less likely to be swayed by lowball offers or gamesmanship.

Here are some general rules on setting the anchor as a function of how much the respective parties know about the subject of the negotiation. These rules aren't cast in stone, so use them only as guidelines. Be prepared to alter your strategy depending on the unique aspects of your negotiation.

- **Other party knows more: More difficult for you to set the anchor, so additional research on your part is necessary to establish your position**
- You know more: Be very aggressive in your anchor position, sending a message to the other party that you're playing hardball
- Both parties know little: Establish aggressive position that isn't excessively demanding, unreasonable, or indefensible
- Both parties know a lot: Anchor carries less weight, it's not as crucial to the eventual outcome, so play it by ear and follow your instincts

This point needs to be hammered home. The first offer is the most important offer you'll ever make. Everything that happens from that point forward, on both sides of the negotiating table, will be based on where the negotiation started. The first offer may be arbitrary with little to no rational basis, so assigning it that much weight seems illogical. It's not about fairness or equity; it's about reality. It's also about strategy and what it will take to get your desired number.

Elementary mathematics plays a pivotal role in the process. If you're the buyer, the higher you start, the less maneuvering room you have to make concessions later. The solution is to start well below where you want to finish and create plenty of upside margin that you can use to trade later.

Once a number has been officially offered or just floated as a trial balloon, it becomes cast in stone by default. While floating a number creates no commitment by either party, it's impossible to retract once disclosed. It becomes part of the backdrop and back-story as the process unfolds. It's analogous to a judge telling the jury to ignore specific testimony they just heard. The reality is that some people will attach even more significance to what was said because they weren't supposed to hear it.

Some buyers are afraid to go first because they might offer more than necessary, such as bidding at an auction. When an item is up for sale, the auctioneer may struggle for the first bid to get things rolling. Once he finds someone brave enough to put their hand in the air with a number, other bidders appear out of the woodwork. None of the subsequent bidders were willing to be first, but they're more than ready to be second, third, or fourth. They fear that if they bid first and no one bids against them, they'll pay more than market value.

This fear also exists in negotiations, and sometimes, you'll get lucky if you don't set the anchor. Assume I have a car I'm willing to sell for $15,000. I park it just off the driveway in front of my house and put a FOR SALE sign on the windshield with no price. A few hours later, I observe a man visually inspecting the vehicle. I step outside to answer his questions and accompany him on a test drive. He likes the car and offers me $18,000 for it. I just picked up $3,000 that I wouldn't have gotten if I'd set the asking price at $15,000. If I'd put it at $20,000, I still would have received $18,000 or perhaps more.

Where you finish a negotiation repeatedly depends on where you start it. Every counteroffer from that point forward will evolve and flow from the starting point. It's critical and consequential that wherever you begin leaves adequate room to negotiate without jeop-ardizing your endgame. If you give away too much too soon, you'll regret it downstream when trying to get closure, and you've run out of bargaining chips. Plan ahead. You'll thank me every time you do.

This section is headlined, "You'll never get it for less than your first offer." That's probably accurate 99% of the time, but as we all know, there are occasional exceptions to everything. I have a case in point that's unusual but worth mentioning because I'm sure it's not unique.

I was interested in an item posted on an online auction website. The asking price was 940 GBP (British pound sterling) with a minimum opening bid of 400 GPB. I submitted a bid of 400 GBP, hoping to be rejected or met with a counteroffer. I intended to pay less, but the online system rejected the lower bids I attempted to submit. So, I had to start at 400 GBP or higher.

I was pleased to receive a counteroffer of 740 GBP. That told me there were no higher bidders than me, an instrumental piece of information since my bid equaled the minimum. Luckily, I could make counteroffers through the auction website email system. Therefore, any counteroffer I made would not be restricted by the minimum initial bid programmed into their software. In response, I submitted my counteroffer of 200 GBP, exactly half of my first bid and the acceptable minimum. I had the leverage I needed because I knew I was the only bidder up to that point.

As a buyer, nothing stops you from making an offer lower than all prior offers. I've done it many times, and the reactions by the other parties ranged from disbelief to outright anger. You know you're over the target when the other side goes ballistic.

The seller sent a message rejecting my offer because it failed to meet the minimum bid requirement of 400 GBP. Furthermore, there would be no counteroffer because I wasn't a serious bidder.

I immediately resubmitted my last offer of 200 GBP with the following narrative: "This is my final offer at this price. Since you have no other bidders, I strongly suggest you accept it within two business days. If you make a counteroffer above my current offer, my next offer will be 100 GBP. Thank you very much for your consideration."

Mission accomplished. Sale price = 200 GBP. Minimum bids are not always what they appear to be.

3. Unless you have a compelling reason not to, always make a counteroffer

When someone offers to buy something I own or sell something I'm interested in, I almost always make a counteroffer, even if we're miles apart on price. It's worth my time, and there's a simple logic behind this approach. It keeps the negotiation open. Otherwise, if I do nothing, the other party may walk away and believe there's no point in continuing the discussion.

There are several reasons why it's a good idea to make a counteroffer. First, it keeps the dialog and interaction going and allows you to collect intelligence about the other party without being obvious. Watch their reaction when you make the offer. What do they say? Are they shocked? Surprised? Happy? Angry? Indignant? Insulted? Also, observe their body movements. All of these are clues that will provide insight as to what your next move might be.

Second, a counteroffer is an excellent way to send a message to the other party without spelling it out. For example, if their asking price is $1,000 and you counteroffer with $500, you're sending a message that they're asking way too much without actually saying it. They obviously wouldn't be happy that you knocked off 50% with one offer, and how they respond will determine the endgame for the negotiation.

If they make a counteroffer significantly under their original asking price, they're conceding they asked for too much and are ready to deal. If they don't make a counteroffer, they're telling you your offer is not within their current window of acceptability. There are an infinite number of ways this could play out. Each successive counteroffer you make should send a message about how far and fast you're willing to move to close the gap. Base the size of your moves to some extent on the succession of moves by the other side.

Third, making a counteroffer takes the pressure off you and puts it back on the other party. You only need to make a relatively small move to accomplish this, and it keeps them engaged. It also signals that you want to deal, but they'll have to provide a substantially more significant offer to keep the process going.

Fourth, there's a possibility the other party needs to make a deal quickly, though they'd lose significant leverage if they disclosed that to you. Experienced negotiators will never give up information that can be used against them, such as pressure from their management to settle or time constraints that require them to sweeten their offers to try and finish the negotiation as soon as possible.

Fifth, making a counteroffer forces the other party to do something, even if it's a rejection or walking away. If I can avoid it, I don't like to keep things hanging with both parties thinking it's the other party's move. That frequently happens, especially when dealing with someone unfamiliar with the process and expecting you to make multiple offers without ever getting a counteroffer from them.

4. Never negotiate against yourself

You're embroiled in a divorce proceeding and attempting to divide the assets without a protracted and costly court battle. You offer your spouse $300,000 to buy him out of his share of the house. He tells you he's insulted by your joke of an offer and that the house is worth infinitely more than that. He's so offended that he won't even make a counteroffer to try and reach an agreement. He tells you to stop wasting his time with ridiculous offers and go back to the drawing board to develop a much bigger number.

His message has shaken you, making you feel like you started much too low. You agonize over whether or not you've jeopardized your ability to settle your differences. You reconsider your position and make him a new offer of $400,000. What have you just done? You negotiated against yourself. You increased your offer without him making an intervening counteroffer.

This exchange is a quintessential example of what not to do in negotiations. Repeat. Never do this, no matter what. I don't care how upset or unglued the other party is about your offer; you do not make another offer under any circumstances until that party has responded to your original offer. It could be an acceptance, rejection, or counteroffer.

During a seminar in Aventura, Florida, for insurance company executives, I showed a slide with only four words: Never negotiate against yourself. After the presentation, one exec approached me to say it was worth coming to the seminar just to hear those four words. He was going through a very traumatic divorce, and at the urging of his lawyer, he'd made several consecutive offers to try and make a deal with his wife. Each offer had been higher than the last, and all were met with her proclaiming that he was cheap, he had undisclosed money and assets she was entitled to, and he was determined to deny her fair share of the settlement. Her lawyer consistently stated there would be a counteroffer only when her husband made a reasonable offer worthy of their consideration.

Predictably, people routinely fall into this trap, and it costs them dearly as a result. Every time you make a new offer without getting a counteroffer, you're conceding money and getting nothing in exchange. Each time you do, it impedes achieving your goal while compounding your opponent's leverage. In this case, millions of dollars were on the line, and he told me he was reaching the end of his rope. He asked me what I would do if I were in his shoes.

I said I'd be more than happy to offer my personal opinion, but not a legal one since we had no attorney-client relationship. First, I'd fire his lawyer (who was getting paid many multiples of hundreds of dollars per hour). Then, I would go back and reinstate my original offer and tell her she had two weeks to accept it or provide a counteroffer. If neither happened, I'd terminate the negotiations and tell her you'll consider any offer they come up with between then and their court date.

Within three months, they forged an agreement after trading a few offers. After wrapping up the details, the exec informed me that the final deal was significantly less than the highest offer submitted before firing his lawyer. Lesson learned. Never make consecutive offers while the other party sits on their hands and does nothing. Drill that into your head so you never make the same mistake he did.

5. Use every scrap of leverage you have and pound it home like there's no tomorrow

A vital component of all negotiations is leverage, which represents a positional advantage grounded in the power to influence actions and events that satisfy your goals and desires. Wealth gives you leverage because it grants you the power to buy whatever you want. Being famous gives you leverage because it grants you access to opportunities unavailable to the average person. For most of us, leverage is harder to come by but no less significant in our daily lives, whether we're negotiating or not.

It's not an overstatement to say that leverage is everything in a negotiation. It's all about leverage. If I enter a negotiation with more leverage than the other party, I'll get what I want at the bottom line. The only way I lose is if I fail to exercise and exploit that leverage to its maximum potential.

To some, leverage may engender an unfavorable connotation because you're intentionally capitalizing on a real or imagined advantage over the other party. Is there something unethical about using that advantage to strike a better deal and achieve your objectives?

For example, if I know someone is about to lose their house in foreclosure because they've been unable to sell it, should I feel guilty about using that knowledge and making a lowball offer that I wouldn't otherwise make? If I manufacture jet aircraft and know that General Electric's current engine orders will be completed next month, that tells me they need new orders to keep their production line going. Is there a reason I shouldn't use that knowledge to drive a hard bargain for my next engine order?

How you use leverage is an individual decision made on a case-by-case basis. My experience in business negotiations is that every advantage will be exploited to the maximum extent possible. If you don't do it, the other side certainly will. There's nothing improper about capitalizing on your advantages in a negotiation to the other party's detriment. That's the whole idea. Otherwise, why are you engaged in a negotiation to begin with? Why not just agree to whatever terms the other party dictates and be done with it?

Leverage is a visible manifestation of experience, knowledge, credibility, resources, power, and outside forces. If you possess these factors entering a negotiation, you've set yourself up for a positive result. These ingredients won't always align in your favor, so it's up to you to compensate for such shortfalls.

Understanding the details of what you're negotiating is essential, especially if the other party is an expert. Unless you're a car enthusiast, the dealership salesman will know more about cars than you do. As a potential buyer, your job is to learn as much as possible about the vehicles that interest you before hitting the car lot. Investing your time in advance will pay off later. Knowledge is powerful, especially for higher-priced items with more room to negotiate.

Credibility is earned over time and is a precious asset. Develop a reputation as someone who presents sound, logical arguments and is willing to listen attentively to the other side's position. You're advocating for a position they disagree with, and hammering them over the head with it isn't productive. You'll be far better off if you come across as sincere, believable, and true to your word.

Having substantial resources behind you is significant when you're a buyer since it allows you to negotiate without concern for financing purchases. Cash buyers of real estate yield much greater leverage than those who have to apply for a mortgage and wait for approval, which may never come. In addition, paying cash will often motivate the seller to accept a lower price in exchange for a quick closing with no hassles or obstacles to derail the process.

Those who occupy senior positions in government and the private sector derive power from their roles and the people they can associate with at the top of the food chain. Power entitles them to certain benefits and perquisites unavailable to the general public. Exercising their privileges frequently includes influencing others to accomplish tasks for them and currying favor with people who can make things happen. If you're trying to get something done and constantly running into roadblocks, people in positions of power can apply leverage where others can't.

Sometimes, power derives from stipulating what you won't do. If you're working with a real estate agent to buy a house, the agent will ask what you can afford to spend on it. Never disclose your budget, regardless of what you're buying. Establishing a budget puts an arbitrary upper limit on what you can buy. You want to buy the best product you can with the money you have to spend. The way you do that is to identify what you want and pay the price you're willing to pay, and you get there by negotiating like a pro.

The danger is buying an inferior product to fit your budget when you could have done much better. Don't let that happen to you. I dedicated a chapter to purchasing a house, providing details on what information to share and what should remain private.

The concept of outside forces influencing negotiations applies equally to everyone because those forces are beyond our control. A prime example of this is the housing market, which is highly dependent on the state of the economy. When economic conditions are good, it's usually a seller's market as prices often rise. When conditions are bad, it's usually a buyer's market as prices often fall.

Another variable is mortgage rates that fluctuate due to prevailing economic factors such as inflation. Additional outside forces impacting negotiations are the ongoing political climate, supply and demand for certain products, changing world events, buyer and seller schedule priorities, weather conditions, and consumer sentiment. Your foremost mission is to capitalize on outside forces when they're favorable to your objectives.

The last thing you want to do is forfeit leverage you can't regain. For example, if I'm shopping for a new car, I won't tell the salesman

I must buy a car that day. Any salesman who hears that is licking his chops at the prospect of closing a sale to a guaranteed customer. You just handed him all the power and whatever leverage you had along with it.

As a buyer, shop around, check out a few cars, and never divulge how much you like a specific vehicle. Keep the salesman in the dark while asking questions about each car and pointing out features that don't appeal to you. This tactic will motivate him to provide as much positive information as possible, giving you details you might never have been aware of. That puts you in the best position to decide whether to purchase, without disclosing your interest. Don't zero in on a favorite until you decide to make an offer. I dedicated a chapter to buying a car and the approaches I recommend to score the best deal.

The first book credited to Donald Trump is *The Art of the Deal*. Often touted as a popular book about negotiating, I'd always wondered why the title isn't *The Art of Negotiating*. When I finally decided to read it, I discovered the book really is about dealmaking and is aptly titled. I found scant information in the book that would help me in a traditional negotiation, so calling it a book about negotiating would be a stretch.

So, what's the difference between making deals and negotiating? The answer, which is strictly my opinion, is leverage. Trump goes through several examples of deals he's cut over the years in great detail. In virtually every example, he held significant and sometimes overpowering leverage over the person he was dealing with that allowed him to dictate the terms of the deal. I noted a considerable scarcity of genuine give-and-take in several of his transactions. That's not a criticism because it's an enviable position to be in whenever possible.

He often bought real estate from people who needed to sell it because they experienced financial distress. The owners were looking for a way out, and Trump was happy to oblige if they met his terms and conditions. When you possess that kind of power and control, it's not a negotiation in a traditional sense. You're not using the skills needed when the leverage between the two parties is relatively balanced. Many of Trump's deals were comparatively one-sided, which helps explain why he had so much success. Business is business, and his eponymously named company is a testament to that success.

I can draw a bright line between dealmaking and negotiating because it's all about the power of superior leverage. Trump had so much leverage most of the time that he rarely faced the challenge of a long, drawn-out, back-and-forth negotiation. Utilizing his approach in negotiations is difficult without that kind of leverage.

Trump's reputation as a skilled, hard-nosed real estate developer works to his advantage because people are apt to seek him out to make deals that otherwise might not get done. His book provides examples of how some of these deals came about and the tactics he executed to close them. He's known for anchoring down by making lowball offers and hanging tough until the other side capitulates. He has amassed a long and successful track record, proving it worked effectively.

Look for leverage in every negotiation. If you can't find it, create it. If you can't create it, make the other party believe you have it. Much of your negotiating power derives from achieving a psychological advantage that can take various forms. For example, significant leverage materializes if the other party believes they have something substantial to lose if there's no deal.

Aside from a potential financial loss, other intangible losses such as prestige, dominance in the marketplace, and self-confidence are at risk. To a large degree, negotiating power is a function of the relative attractiveness to each side of not reaching an agreement. Ideally, you always want the other party to need a deal more than you do and make them pay for it.

6. "Compromise" doesn't mean I'll meet you halfway

I don't like the word "compromise." It signifies weakness and that you're willing to sacrifice your principles for something you might not otherwise get. It's an admission that logic and common sense failed to prevail. It's tempting to think that nothing would ever get done if people never compromised. After all, agreements won't happen if both sides in a dispute refuse to budge from their respective positions. That certainly sounds reasonable, and I hear it all the time. It's a myth.

I never walk into a negotiation seeking a compromise, and I never start negotiations with that word in my vocabulary. It projects vulnerability, unsureness, timidity, and a willingness to abandon your bedrock principles. Don't take this the wrong way. I'm not saying you'll consistently get everything you want in a negotiation. There's always going to be some give-and-take to reach a handshake eventually. The point is that you don't start with the idea that compromise is inevitable and conclude with concessions that are crucial to you. Rather than looking for compromise, focus your sights and energy on collaboration.

Many people struggle to overcome this hurdle because serious negotiations sometimes require confrontation. I know many people who dislike confrontation because they experience so much of it in their daily lives. Why invite more of it into your life when you don't have to?

One way to minimize confrontation is to seek compromise, which is the last thing on my mind during a tough negotiation. I don't negotiate to compromise; I do it to get what I want when I want it. I say that unequivocally. Negotiation is not a marriage that requires compromise to survive. When two people live in one home, there will be plenty of tie votes, which explains why the Supreme Court has an odd number of justices. There are no tie votes.

If you start negotiations in a posture that compromise is a viable plan of attack, then there is no attack. You've already conceded some leverage you might otherwise use to squeeze the other party into submission. Leverage is your most formidable weapon in every negotiation. Never relinquish a smidgeon of it without substantial concessions from the other party.

If there's a time for compromise, it's in the closing stages of a negotiation after you've executed your plan and need a way to shrink the final gap. Splitting the difference should be averted whenever possible, but sometimes the difference in positions is so slight that both sides relent and agree to share it equally. I've done it when it became clear that the time of all the people involved was worth more than haggling over the last few dollars separating us. The unmistakable danger is that too many people choose this approach prematurely and find themselves trapped with no viable escape route.

Let's assume you're negotiating a contract, and you've reached a point where you're $2 million apart. You're the buyer at $49 million, and the seller is at $51 million. If you propose to split the difference to close the deal at $50 million, there's nothing to stop the seller from countering with a double-split between that $50 million and their $51 million and settling at $50.5 million. They'd treat your $50 million as an offer rather than a settlement amount to end the negotiation. That would put you in a position of closing 75% of the original difference, with only 25% attributed to the seller. That's not a favorable outcome for you, so I always wait for the other party to propose a split from their last offer. That way, they're making two consecutive offers while I haven't moved an inch. It also allows me to reject the split and continue negotiating.

There are several old parables involving oranges, but one in particular is relevant to the type of mindset that can determine success or failure in a negotiation. Two people claim ownership of the same orange, so they settle their dispute by compromising and cutting it in half. They later discover that one wanted the juice and the other wanted the rind, but it was too late, so neither party got what they wanted.

Avoiding this flawed outcome was incredibly simple. Both parties needed to communicate their intentions rudimentarily to ensure they understood why they were there. This process should happen at the beginning of every negotiation while addressing this question: What are we here to negotiate, and what do both sides expect to achieve?

At the same time, keep your negotiation strategy and price goal to yourself. You want to determine if there's a viable way to solve a dispute or disagreement by stepping back and reviewing where both sides stand at the outset. There's a reasonable chance of some commonality between you, but it must be exposed. You may discover the framework for an agreement is possible without a protracted battle of wills. In this example of the orange, skilled negotiators could have easily satisfied both parties in a matter of minutes.

The prevailing tendency in negotiations is to focus on the respective positions and differences between the opposing parties. So, I'm here, and you're way over there. How do we close that gap? Instead, initially focus on shared interests. You want to sell your car. I want to buy your car. At the top level, we have a common goal: Transferring its ownership. Initiate a process of identifying the aspects of the vehicle that are not at issue. After completing that process, there's no point in engaging in a price negotiation if the buyer determines that he's no longer interested in it or if the seller wants to disengage for some reason.

Find out what you have in common before you delve into what's driving you apart. Unexposed facts and information can lay the foundation for an agreement, even if the price is still in contention. As mentioned previously, price should be the last thing you discuss. Keeping price off the table is often difficult because you can't control the other party's actions. Price may be the only thing they want to talk about. Learn how to deflect away from that discussion by refocusing on all the elements of the bargain.

I used a variation of this approach when I handled the distribution of my parent's estate to my four brothers and me. Many sentimental heirlooms from their home had been given to us over the years to minimize the overall tax burden, but their house was still brimming with furniture and art when my father died. His instructions were to sell everything that remained and equally divide the proceeds. I knew there were things my brothers and I wanted, but I had little insight into who wanted what.

Rather than attempt to hash it out as a group, I asked each to independently make a list of the items they'd like to have, understanding they'd have to buy them from the estate. I was using a bit of psychology with this approach. Keeping these lists independent might lessen the chances that we'd all go after some of the same items. I was attempting to avoid the pile-on effect. There's no way to prove this happens because you can't go back and redo everything to see how it would have turned out otherwise. I was playing the odds the way I saw them.

I put together my list without seeing the other four. Amazingly, the lists contained no duplicate items. I did appraisals on the combined list, and we all got our selected items. We had no battles, and everyone was happy with the results. While finding areas where you agree is always advisable, it benefits everyone to avoid areas where you might disagree.

Did I get lucky with the way this turned out? Maybe. After all, the chances that our lists would all be completely different were minimal. Even if there were a few duplicates, I knew we could focus on those items, having already settled the rest. It was worth a shot, and the results back that up.

7. Always be prepared to walk away, and not necessarily as a last resort

The decision to walk out on a negotiation is major, should never be taken lightly, and is sometimes an act of last resort when nothing else seems to be working. Consider it a potent tactic that can often make or break a negotiation.

Walking out on a negotiation is a tactical move, not a strategic one. When you walk, you do it confidently and purposefully and never look back. You're not bluffing. The goal is to send a clear, powerful, unspoken message to the other side that the negotiation is dead in the water. While the specific circumstances for the stalemate will vary, they'll share a common dilemma. The other party refuses to negotiate in good faith, and staying engaged would only waste more of your valuable time.

If called back on your way out the door, you should politely return and say nothing. If asked why you left so abruptly, tell them exactly what was implied by your unexpected departure. If that fails to get their attention, say, "Let me know when you're serious about continuing these negotiations." Don't be held hostage to their unwillingness to forge ahead in good faith. It's a dramatic step but loses its effectiveness if you do it more than once during a negotiation.

Walking away is an exceptionally viable tactic when your leverage is substantially greater than your opponent's, such as when buying a car. There are usually several dealers and private sellers to choose from, and all other things being equal, you're likely to buy at the lowest price. Researching and shopping around will put you in a position to strike the best deal.

If you show up at a car dealership with enough cash to buy the car you've chosen, you're the last person they want to leave their lot without taking your money, only to have the next dealer take it. If they won't agree to the deal you seek and there's no convincing reason to buy from that dealer, it's a good time to walk. Feel free to negotiate simultaneously with multiple parties before signing an agreement.

The Best Alternative To a Negotiated Agreement (BATNA) is a term of art used to determine a favorable decision risk profile for walking away. It presumes that you only negotiate to get something better than your best alternative to no deal. If an alternative is as good or better than what you're attempting to negotiate, there's no compelling reason to deal. However, if you decide to negotiate, you always have the BATNA in your hip pocket as a fallback position. That's potent leverage because it allows you to walk away or terminate the negotiation at any point with few to no consequences.

The BATNA will also help you avoid making snap decisions due to intimidation attempts by the other party and prepare you to fend off their most robust tactics without emotion or uncertainty. If the other party threatens to walk away, objectively explain both sides' current circumstances and the actions you'll institute to implement your BATNA if necessary. This technique puts the other party on notice that you want to continue negotiations, but you're fully prepared should they break down.

Before you start negotiating, assume you have the following three endgames available: (1) no deal, (2) assuming there is no deal, your best alternative to no deal, and (3) a deal that's better than your best alternative to no deal. Since your working assumption is that you only negotiate for #3, you must determine what #2 is before doing anything else.

If you find yourself at an impasse and decide your proposed deal is better than no deal for the other party, that gives you powerful leverage, and it's a good time to walk. It would be foolish for the other party to reject a deal that's better than nothing. It happens, but not often. The more leverage you have in this situation, the less likely they'll let you walk away. You need to know how important it is for them to secure a deal and the impact if that doesn't happen. Through prior research and probing questions, a skilled negotiator will assemble enough information to ascertain what the opponent will likely do under a few potential scenarios.

As noted earlier, negotiating power is a function of the relative attractiveness to each side of not reaching an agreement. This alternate way of assessing leverage requires you to analyze what you're doing from the inside out. If not reaching an agreement is of little consequence to you, and you can easily live without one, be patient and use that adaptability to your advantage. Your power is inversely proportional to your need to get a deal, so don't hesitate to walk away if the other side isn't coming around to your way of thinking. Leverage is king, and always be willing to squeeze them when circumstances and relevant facts align with your negotiating position. If walking away is the best option in your judgment, do it.

Finding your BATNA requires thinking outside the box and exploring opportunities you didn't initially consider. It's worth the time and effort to dig in and identify as many viable options as possible to maximize your interests as you move forward. This can be a complex process that involves trade-offs besides price. Schedule, warranties, maintenance, desirability, and reputation can also play a role in such decisions. Integrate these factors to provide an apples-to-apples comparison for you to evaluate and rank. The answer isn't always clear, but do whatever you can to isolate your best options.

Many negotiators start with a "bottom line" that they won't violate. At least, that's what they promise themselves. They won't go above a certain number if they're a buyer and won't go below a certain number if they're a seller. The theory is that if you don't establish a line in the sand at the outset, you're more predisposed to weaken and wobble as the negotiation progresses and undermine your objective. It's like walking into a casino and promising you won't gamble more than $500. Once you hit your limit, you stop no matter what. If you don't, you're afraid that $500 soon turns into $1,000, which turns into $2,000. Before you know it, you've blown your monthly mortgage and car payments.

Your BATNA is not a bottom line or a line in the sand. Drawing a line in the sand limits your options as the negotiation unfolds. Negotiations are dynamic, requiring you to adapt to changing conditions and assumptions you didn't anticipate. Don't adopt a rigid position from which you can't extract yourself as you attempt to gain a tactical advantage. What you thought was realistic yesterday may not be practical today. Locking yourself in and focusing on one arbitrary number hinder your creative thought process and ability to arrive at the best number possible.

Determining your BATNA at the beginning allows you to take full advantage of its power and establishes a baseline for measuring all other possible deals. Your BATNA may change over time, which gives you added leverage as it improves. If better alternatives arise as the negotiation progresses, evaluate and integrate them into your strategic plan. A well-conceived BATNA acts as a sword and shield to protect you during the heat of battle and help you make sound risk/reward decisions when enduring the stress and pressure of a tough negotiation.

8. Make the other party earn and pay for every concession you make

The principle of making them pay is routinely violated when the other party gets mad because you've insulted them with an offer far below their expectations. You feel guilty and decide they might have a point, so you make a bigger concession than you had initially planned. As soon as you do it, you kick yourself when you realize you've violated one of the cardinal rules of negotiating. You never give anything away without calculated resistance and a clear-cut plan to get something of equal or better value in return.

There's a barefaced reason why casinos use chips instead of cash at their gambling tables. While convenience, uniformity, security, and data collection play a role, the principal reason is purely psychological. It's demonstrably easier to separate a gambler from his chips than from his cold, hard cash. They're only chips, after all, and although the dollar denominations feature different colors, they're the same size and weight. So, it's just as easy to throw down a $100 bet as it is to throw down a $5 bet. You don't have to laboriously count your cash before placing your bet because the chips have already done that for you.

Counting cash requires you to focus on every bill to make sure it's the amount you intended. The more bills you dig out and sort through to make a bet, the more you realize this is your hard-earned money on the line. With chips, you only have to pick the colors, and off you go. It's a mindless exercise. With a couple of chips, you can bet as much as an entire wad of cash. You're inclined to risk more money if you don't see "real" money leaving your hand. In a visual sense, a couple of chips immersed in a sea of green felt amazingly doesn't look like much. Combine this sensory phenomenon with the intoxicating sound of chips being stacked and restacked, along with players incessantly shuffling them with one hand, and you have the perfect formula for a continuous flow of money into the house coffers.

When trading offers in a negotiation, money takes on a symbolism eerily similar to a casino chip. I'll make the case that you're even more vulnerable in a negotiation because you don't use anything material to represent money visibly, and actual money only changes hands once the deal is sealed. So, as the offers and counteroffers go back and forth either verbally or in writing, it's easier to part with your money because you don't witness it physically exiting your bank account. Purge that casino mentality from your head whenever you're negotiating, or you'll find yourself casually making concessions for no valid reason.

Legend has it that the expression "If you scratch my back, I'll scratch yours" originated with the British Royal Navy in the 17th century. The ships had strict rules against drunkenness and disobedience, and punishments were often severe. One method involved tying the guilty sailor to the ship's mast and flogging him with a lash. Crew members often collaborated, so the whippings only resulted in light scratches on their backs. They knew they'd be treated similarly if they ever found themselves on the wrong end of the lash.

In a legal sense, the applicable term of art is "quid pro quo," the Latin expression that means "something for something" or "one thing for another." In an ideal world, what you give up would be of equal value to what you receive in return. However, in the world of negotiation, my goal is to always end up with more than I gave up and not just by a small amount. If I concede anything, I expect compensation that puts me in a better position than when I started. That's easier said than done, but you'll only get there if you set the bar high enough to create a challenge. I'll make the other party pay top dollar for every concession I make.

Concede grudgingly and with appropriate resistance for the offered compensation. Move incrementally and slowly. Don't foster the impression that you've got a lot more in the tank before it's empty. Instead, you want the other party to sense genuine pain on your part for each concession you make. If it looks too easy, they'll keep wanting more and more. Save one final concession for the endgame to incentivize the other party to close the deal. It should be something you know they want and big enough to strike a nerve without jeopardizing your objective. Try to figure that out at the beginning of negotiations and save it for when you need it.

Patience is one of your best weapons, especially if the other party is anxious to get a deal. The more time it takes them to extract a concession from you, the more likely they'll make relatively bigger concessions in return. Patience pays, and to illustrate how true that is, here's an example from almost two decades ago.

I was searching for a used compact crossover sport utility vehicle like the Toyota RAV4 (recreational active vehicle with four-wheel drive). I searched online and found what I was looking for at a dealership close to home, so I drove over to take a look. It's tricky to casually look at cars on a dealer's lot because the salesmen are on a mission to sell you one, and they let you know it. I discreetly checked out several cars without flagging the one I was interested in. I went inside to make an offer on the RAV4 I wanted, conditioned on a test drive and independent maintenance assessment.

I sat down with a salesman and told him the asking price of $23,000 was far too much to pay based on my research. I offered $15,000 cash with no trade-in, a 35% reduction from his price. He chuckled and suggested I didn't know what I was talking about. His reaction was precisely what I was hoping for. I obviously hadn't offered more than it was worth. So far, so good.

Our discussion continued for quite some time, and before long, he was joined by the sales manager, followed by the assistant manager of the dealership. Now, we might make some progress, but they refused to make a counteroffer. I told them to call me if they changed their minds, and we'd meet at a neutral location to negotiate a deal. They committed the cardinal sin of auto sales and let me walk away without spending a dime.

A few weeks later, I bought a different car in a private sale, but I wanted to keep an eye on that RAV4 I'd looked at. Things got interesting rather quickly. I checked the dealer's website a month later, and they'd dropped the price from $23,000 to $21,000. It fell to $19,000 the following month and the month after that to $18,000. When it dropped to $17,000 a month later, I called the dealership and asked to speak to the assistant manager. I told him who I was and reminded him I'd offered $15,000 a few months earlier and was laughed out of the building. I told him I was willing to push my offer up to $17,000 then, but no one would negotiate with me. Now you're offering the car for $17,000 and still have no buyer. So, who's laughing now?

Meanwhile, that RAV4 had been occupying space on their lot for months, preventing it from being used to sell other vehicles. There's also an overhead expense associated with cars for sale, since they need periodic cleaning and mechanical checks to ensure everything is still working as advertised. I didn't rub in their bungled mishandling of a potential sale because I didn't need to. The manager readily admitted they'd dropped the ball and was disappointed to learn I'd already bought another car. I thanked him for his time and told him my patience had saved me once again.

There's an old adage that it's not what you say but how you say it that matters. While both are important in negotiations, delivery and tone of voice can be more potent weapons than content. Establishing a meaningful connection is crucial, or the content will likely go in one ear and out the other. A straightforward way to do this is to look people directly in the eye when you talk to them. Many people don't do this, and the impression one gets is they're distracted and talking at the person rather than to them. It's also disrespectful to look at your notes or computer screen while speaking, except for occasional seconds to refresh your memory. Either look me in the eye or don't talk to me.

One of the best ways to break down communication barriers is to tell a good story. People relate to stories better than logical arguments and remember stories more easily than facts and figures. The story can be about something unrelated to the negotiation but illustrates a point or principle relevant to the discussion. I've included a few short examples elsewhere in this book. One is about splitting an orange in half, which leaves both sides unsatisfied. Another is about the pessimist and the optimist and how personal demeanor can drive dispute resolutions. I also included a couple about President "Silent Cal" Coolidge.

Self-awareness, mannerisms, and appearance definitely matter. How you project to the other side depends on many things, but they'll be impacted more by how you feel than how you think. Those impressions will also stay with them much longer and greatly influence how they react to what you say.

9. Only negotiate with someone empowered to commit

Before negotiating, ensure the other party is fully empowered to make binding commitments. When you meet for the first time, ask them if they have that power. You'll typically get one of two answers if they work for a company and negotiate on its behalf. Either they or someone higher in their chain of command has the power.

If it's a small business, chances are you'll be dealing with the owner, president, or someone responsible for handling contractual matters on behalf of the company. It's usually a straightforward process to determine who can sign for the company and who can't.

With medium to large companies, who you deal with often depends on the size of the negotiation relative to the company's overall business. I do my best to avoid situations where the nego-tiation results are subject to review by a higher authority in the company. If I'm dealing with a relatively large company and the only person who can bind that company is the president or CEO, I probably won't get that person in the room with me. In that event, I'll request a delegation letter signed by the president that grants temporary authority to a subordinate to negotiate on his behalf.

A manager in the contracts, purchasing, or subcontracts depart-ment will most likely receive such a delegation. Ensure their author-ity covers up to the dollar amount anticipated for your negotiation. If you doubt whether the assigned person has the requisite authority, request that they provide the evidence.

There's a clearly defined chain of command when dealing with the federal government. Contracting Officers (KO) can legally bind the U.S. government to a contract of higher value than the micro-purchase amount of $10,000. Agency heads can issue Cer-tificates of Appointment that delegate and define the scope of authority granted by the warrant, which usually includes the power to negotiate, execute, modify, and terminate a contract. Contract administrators and specialists sometimes negotiate less complex and costly contracts but can't bind the government. Verify the existence of any such delegation with the KO before proceeding.

If it's a personal negotiation and you're the buyer, ensure you're dealing with the owner or his authorized representative. For example, if you're buying a car in a private sale, ask the seller to produce the legal title. If the seller represents the owner as their agent to sell the vehicle, ask for a delegation letter signed by the owner that grants the required authority to the representative. If it's a sizeable dollar-value item, take it further and personally verify the authorization with the owner. There's no benefit to shaking hands with someone thinking you have a deal, only to find out later that the person you were dealing with didn't have the power to make the deal.

Avoid potential problems before they happen. Never put yourself in a position where you're negotiating with someone not empowered to commit to and enforce an agreement. Agreements made by company employees are usually reviewed and approved by upper management. You need advance assurances that this type of review won't change the price and would only affect the outcome if the employee agreed to something they consider illegal, unethical, or provably impossible for the company to perform. In other words, company management can't order a do-over on price because they don't like the result. Without such assurances, you put yourself in the position of wasting valuable time and getting nothing in return.

This discussion is slightly off topic but worthy of attention should a negotiation go off the rails and a settlement is hopeless. Suppose you have a personal dispute with a retailer that won't honor its merchandise return policy. The retailer says your item is ineligible for return under the policy, and you say it is. Despite your best efforts to settle the dispute amicably, the customer service department won't budge. Furthermore, store management has reviewed the matter and has reaffirmed that position. As far as the store is concerned, it's over. Case closed.

You can take action that I've used on a couple of occasions. You can file suit in small claims court for the item's value, filing fees, incidental costs, and any legal expenses incurred. Recovery of specific costs will depend on the state law where the suit is filed. Before doing that, however, I highly recommend you tell the retailer you plan to bring suit against it. It should not be an idle threat and should not be directed at a store clerk or customer service representative. Direct that message only to someone in the company who has the requisite position and power to react to it. Otherwise, you're wasting time with an employee who's simply a messenger.

It may not be apparent who in the company should be told of your plan to sue. If the retailer is a small business with one location, target the owner of the business. If it's a big company like Walmart, I'd target the store manager. If you're dissatisfied with his reaction to your warning, I'd go straight to the corporate president and CEO with a formal letter that describes the dispute in detail. These warnings would all precede the filing of a lawsuit.

In every instance where I've threatened to sue or filed suit, I got what I wanted without going to court. There's one requisite caution. My claims were well-founded, and I had convincing evidence to substantiate them. Companies don't want to spend money on highly-paid lawyers to fight small consumer claims that could generate bad publicity, but if your claim is frivolous and unsupported, you can expect them to fight back. If you lose, whatever time and money you've spent up to that point pursuing your claim is a sunk cost you'll never recover.

In conclusion, I will only negotiate with people who make commitments they can keep. I want to avoid finding myself in a position where I believe I've struck a deal, only to discover my agreement is subject to the approval of someone who had nothing to do with the actual process. How I deal with that depends on the individual situation. Still, I won't proceed with a negotiation if I discover contingencies or limitations to the power of the individual I'm dealing with.

Nothing substantive or productive will happen until this critical component is buttoned up and resolved. Unfortunately, too often, this isn't done because people assume whoever's in the room wouldn't be there if they didn't possess the power to negotiate. Don't assume anything. Always take the time to establish and verify the credentials of those you're dealing with.

10. Negotiate on friendly turf whenever possible

In negotiating, there's such a thing as home-field advantage. With few exceptions, you're better off negotiating at your place of business, your home, or another suitable venue that's close and convenient to you. There's no reason to let the other party dictate where a negotiation occurs, but they will if you let them. I guarantee that I will.

Home field is highly valued in sports, yet people routinely give that advantage away when buying things like a car. It doesn't occur to most people that this powerful tool is available to them like it is to a sports team. To understand and appreciate this advantage's potential impact, let's look at an example that almost everyone can relate to.

You're shopping for a new or used car at a local dealer. After arriving, it doesn't take long for a salesman to acquire his target and ask what you're looking for. Let's assume you find a car that interests you and decide to make an offer. Unless you're shopping at a Rolls-Royce, Lamborghini, or other high-end dealership, you'll be ushered into a small office or cubicle and offered a seat and a beverage. At that point, the process many people dread begins.

If the salesman has difficulty making a deal, you'll first get a visit from the sales manager. Next, you'll see his boss if things still aren't progressing. You may be feeling uncomfortable by now, and while everyone is very polite and businesslike, you sense pressure to make something happen. Your discomfort is a direct result of the salesman operating on friendly turf.

The salesman occupying the high ground is no accident. It doesn't have to be that way, but most people shopping for a car put themselves through it nonetheless. Why? Because that's the way it's always been done, and dealers aren't about to change it. There's no reason why you can't change it, given that they want to sell you a car, and most salesmen work at least partially on commission.

When you're close to making a decision, tell the salesman you want to think it over, and you'll call to set up a meeting at

Starbucks or a similar neutral venue to discuss the transaction and review relevant documents. If you're comfortable with the idea, invite the salesman to your home for coffee and snacks. That puts you squarely in the power seat and removes him from his comfort zone. His access to reinforcements is limited to phone calls and electronic messages. You've secured the ultimate home-field advantage to drive the bargain you want.

Quickly establish this negotiating edge whenever possible. If you're buying a boat in a private sale at someone's home, the seller has the advantage and has no reason to give that up by moving the vessel. When companies negotiate with each other, it's commonplace for the buyer to insist on meeting at their place of business. A seller risks losing a potential sale if they attempt to change the location against the buyer's wishes.

While there aren't legions of devoted fans cheering from the sidelines of a negotiation, there are reasons why friendly turf is beneficial that go beyond the distinct advantages in sports. In many of my business negotiations, there were occasions where issues arose that required the input of specialists to resolve. Those specialists are immediately available if you're meeting at your company's place of business, and they're far more effective if they appear personally rather than by telephone or teleconference. These may be the only options for the other party if they've flown in from another state unless they decide to put their expert on a plane so that he can attend in person.

Friendly turf provides the convenience of bringing in key support personnel in real time. I've witnessed this often and observed that remotely-held negotiations have limits. My preference is to conduct face-to-face negotiations whenever feasible. Business negotiations at your company location also keep you home rather than a hotel room away from family and friends.

One downside of negotiating on friendly turf is that you're expected to perform your regular job duties regardless of how much time you spend in negotiations. Depending on your circumstances, this can be a major distraction if the burden becomes too great. With the growing trend of working remotely, this burden can extend to both parties if negotiations are conducted online.

11. Everything is always on sale, until it isn't

Have you ever been on a cruise to the Caribbean Islands? Make a stop at most ports, and you'll see tourists scurrying around the local shops. They have a common desire to wheel and deal with the shop owners to get the best bargain possible. The same people paying sticker prices at home will get off their ship and negotiate for everything they buy in a gift shop. They'll do this even if the total of everything they buy is less than $100.

One reason they'll provide for doing this is that, unlike at home, island merchants expect you to deal with them. So, if you don't, you'll pay a lot more than you had to, and the merchant will laugh all the way to the bank. Based on my personal experience, they're right. Negotiating is a way of life in many parts of the world and within certain cultures.

I've always marveled at this phenomenon because these people rarely act the same way in the U.S. They walk into any retail store and routinely pay the marked price without blinking an eye. Why aren't they wheeling and dealing in their home country while never hesitating to do it elsewhere? Why do they almost always assume they can't negotiate? What's going on here?

Fans of the television show *Seinfeld* are no strangers to the dysfunctional tribulations of its four main characters making their way in New York City. Many episodes feature extended back-and-forth discussions about their daily lives that don't always appear to be negotiations in a traditional sense. However, the opening scene of "The Chicken Roaster" episode during season eight reveals George asking the same question I just posed regarding our collective failure to negotiate.

The show begins with George and Jerry standing on the sidewalk outside a market that sells fresh fruits and vegetables. When the dialog starts, George is holding a bottle of orange drink he's thinking about buying.

George: "Dollar eighty-nine. Why is this a dollar eighty-nine? Why is there no haggling in this country?"

Jerry: "I guess we like to think we've progressed beyond a knife fight for a citrus drink."

George: "Not me. Everything should be negotiable."

Jerry: "Restaurants, too?"

George: "Absolutely. You're telling me there's no room to move on pasta? All starches are a scam."

Jerry: "Yeah, especially ziti with that big hole."

George, holding a container of ziti pasta, addresses the store manager: "Excuse me, how much is this?"

Manager: "Dollar nineteen."

George: "I'll give you a quarter."

Manager: "Get the hell out of here!"

Jerry: "Tell him forty and no fork."

George: "Thirty."

Manager: "That's it, you leave and never come back!"

Jerry: "How about we leave and come back in a week?"

Manager: "Deal!"

George: "Alright, see? We got something there."

When his ridiculous first offer is rejected, I compliment George on exhibiting the right mindset and not buckling. While I'd never haggle over the price of a $1.19 container of ziti pasta, we should not assume we can't negotiate. Once you make that assumption, you've conceded everything to the other side. Don't close that door without at least attempting to open it.

The reality is that almost everything in life is negotiable, both in business and your personal life, no matter how large or small the cost. We all conduct hundreds of negotiations every day without always realizing it. The vast majority of them are nontraditional because they don't necessarily involve a buyer and seller haggling over price. However, when it comes to traditional negotiations, the American people have been conditioned to negotiate under a very narrow set of ground rules and circumstances.

They act like programmed robots trained to pay sticker prices for less expensive items than a house or car. Has it ever occurred to them they've got nothing to lose by making an offer that chops off a nice chunk of that price? In addition, items marked down as part of an advertised sale are sitting ducks for lowball offers that undercut the "sale" prices. The sale and clearance prices are often arbitrarily assigned, and there's nothing to prevent you from offering whatever you want.

Prices are not cast in stone. Adopt an attitude that everything is on sale until it isn't. The seller's profit margins propel a few exceptions to this rule of thumb. For example, I don't expect to negotiate in a grocery store or supermarket. They operate on slim margins and generate profit on volume, so I always pay sticker prices.

Similar logic applies to the big-box retailers that rely on volume to offset lower prices. Generally, they won't negotiate because they can't afford to. I'm also not going to negotiate the price of gasoline for my car. Contrary to mainstream media propaganda, gas stations are not gouging you whenever you pull in for a fill-up. Many offer gas as a convenience, so you'll buy snacks and drinks during your stop. That's where they make the lion's share of their profits.

If you walk into a store and willingly pay the sticker price, you'll never know if you could have paid less. Maybe even a lot less. It's rare for a store employee to disclose they'll negotiate, but the last thing you should do is ask them if they will. It's a blaring sign of weakness on your part. It's also a signal to the seller that all they have to do is say no, and you'll scrap the idea of trying to reduce their price.

There's an old saying that when you get ready to do something that might get you into hot water, don't ask for permission but beg for forgiveness if necessary. You fear that asking permission will guarantee a denial. If what you're trying to do is reasonably uncomplicated and straightforward but seems to be snagged in a never-ending bureaucratic morass, you circumvent that roadblock and do what you want without approval. You're gambling that if your misdeed is detected, the penalty will be nowhere near as destructive as waiting for the bureaucracy to come to its senses and grant your request.

Countless times, I've witnessed people ask for permission to negotiate. Why do they assume the seller is in the power seat? You're the one with the money! When I walk into a store, everything is on sale whether the store knows it or not. I never ask permission to do anything. If I decide to make an offer to buy something, I make it. The worst that can happen is they say no, and I've lost absolutely nothing.

Many years ago, my brothers and I needed a new amplifier to power our band's PA system. We visited our favorite music store and found a Peavey amp that meshed nicely with our speakers. The salesman offered a quote, and one of my brothers immediately asked him for his lowest price. The salesman knocked 10% off and said that was the best he could do. We consummated the sale and left the store.

I told my brother that's not the way to negotiate. Asking the salesman for his lowest price established a floor that prevented us from getting an even better deal. That floor became a bright line he could not cross without destroying his credibility. He'd either sell the amp at his lowest price or die on that hill trying. I said the better strategy was to make an offer below our target and force him to accept or reject it. If our offer was in the ballpark of where the salesman could go, the odds were good he'd either accept it or provide a counteroffer.

Making the first offer allows you to set the anchor and test the water on how locked in he is to the asking price. That's the vital insight needed to determine your next move and evaluate how he might respond.

How do you know if someone will negotiate with you? Make an offer and watch what happens. You don't need permission to offer a price different than theirs. There's nothing magical about their price. It's just a number they hope you'll pay without questioning it. If you pay their price, they just took your money without breaking a sweat. It's what negotiators call easy money, and it happens constantly.

When you make an offer, rejection is the worst thing that will happen. You might get laughed at and even be told you insulted the seller by not paying their price. You'll never be an effective negotiator if you don't have the stomach for confrontation and rejection or are overly concerned about the other party's reaction to an offer. If you're concerned they'll think of you as being cheap and stingy with your money and are quick to tell you right to your face, you don't have the iron gut necessary to win.

There's a simple decision to make when dealing with someone who refuses to negotiate. You either pay the asking price or go somewhere else. I always choose the latter if I believe they have maneuvering room within their price. Sometimes, walking away provides enough shock value for the seller to reconsider and continue the discussions. I employed this strategy when I bought my last car. Car salesmen understand that anyone leaving their lot without a purchase is probably a lost opportunity, so they'll exhaust every tactic in the book to hold on to you for as long as possible. Take advantage of your leverage because there will be plenty of times when you have virtually no leverage, and you'll do almost anything to get it.

My father had an aversion to negotiation because he was very easygoing and admittedly nonconfrontational. He never negotiated in the islands because he felt the merchants struggling to make a living needed the money to survive. I told him that many of those merchants made good money at the expense of unsuspecting tourists who were ready to throw their money away. I also reminded him that those merchants set their prices based on the assumption that you'll always negotiate. Lowball offers were expected and planned for, so if you didn't deal with them, you fattened their profit margins. I couldn't persuade him.

During the days when newspapers reigned supreme, and the internet didn't exist, my father would comb through the Sunday edition clipping discount coupons. He'd spend at least an hour amassing coupons that would save him around $10 on his next visit to the supermarket. Despite this extensive effort to save himself $10, he wouldn't hesitate to walk into a store and pay the sticker price for a new television.

When he decided to buy a flatscreen television, I told him I could save him 30 to 40 times that $10 in less than two minutes, and that's exactly what I did. I said it made no sense to spend hours and hours poring through newspapers to save a few bucks with coupons, only to give it back many times over every time he bought something substantial. He's one of many who do this because coupon savings are automatic and require no confrontation. You just hand them over with no negotiation required.

I'm just the opposite. I'm always in standby negotiation mode and prepared to react to whatever comes up. What some might consider a confrontation is a new opportunity for me. I don't pay much attention to coupons because I can save far more by applying my time and energy to consequential savings on big-ticket items.

12. Beware of the warranty trap

When you buy a new product, you expect it will perform its intended function, whether or not a written guarantee covers it. You can return it for a refund or exchange if it doesn't meet the warranty terms. Most retailers reliably live up to their promises and sometimes bend them in favor of the consumer when it makes sense from a business standpoint.

A guarantee is a promise included in a written warranty. The terms "guarantee" and "warranty" are often used interchangeably but consider the warranty as the legally enforceable attestation to a product's quality, durability, and performance. A breach of warranty occurs if a product or service doesn't live up to those promises, resulting in enforceable remedies. Save your warranty documents as a record of coverages, available remedies, and claim procedures.

On rare occasions, I've had disputes with retailers regarding their warranties and exchange policies. These policies, whether written or in digital format, explain the terms and conditions in specific detail. My experience reveals that it sometimes pays to challenge those policies when you deem them unsatisfactory to resolve your problem. Also, be aware that there are implied warranties you may not know about.

Warranties are either express or implied, and it's important to understand the distinction. An express warranty is essentially an insurance policy that covers the replacement or repair of a product. It's specific to that product, defines the types of coverages available, and the period those coverages apply. It usually includes assurances that the product is free from defects in materials and workmanship.

While most warranties originate with the manufacturer, the product service or repair may be delegated to a local dealer or retailer. If you're not satisfied with the warranty service at the local level, take your complaint directly to the manufacturer for resolution. Don't let anyone at the local level discourage you from pursuing your claim if you believe you have a valid case.

While an in-depth discussion of the Uniform Commercial Code (UCC) is well beyond the scope of this book, a basic understanding of Article 2, which deals with sales and contracts, is extremely valuable to small business owners and consumers. Many people are unaware that even if there is no express warranty, certain implied warranties apply to merchants engaged in the sale of products. These warranties are enforceable by the consumer even though they aren't provided in writing. The UCC applies in most states, but check your state for specifics.

These warranties are important because many things you buy don't have an express warranty. For example, when you purchase food and beverages, you expect them to be fresh and safe to eat up to their expiration date if they have one. Failure to meet those criteria results in a full refund.

The implied "warranty of merchantability" guarantees that products are merchantable and fit for their intended purpose. Implied warranties don't cancel or replace express warranties but extend above and beyond any existing warranties. They assure consumers that the products sold are of equal quality and value to similar goods. The warranty presumes the consumer will use the products in their intended manner and they will meet his reasonable expectations based on the merchant's representations.

Sometimes, you go into a store to buy something you're unfamiliar with. You may have a basic understanding of the product but need more detailed information before deciding if and what you'll purchase. You're apt to consult with someone in the store who's knowledgeable about the product and ask questions. When you rely on that employee's expertise in choosing what to buy, an implied "warranty of fitness for a particular purpose" attaches to that transaction. The seller doesn't have to be a merchant in this case but must know your intended use for the product.

Let's assume you want to take up fly fishing and know little about it. You go to the nearest store that sells all the gear you'll need. You engage with someone in sales who explains the various equipment, and based on his recommendations, you select a rod, reel, boots, waders, net, and other items that he suggests. He knows what you plan to do with everything you buy, so there's an implied warranty that those items fit their intended purpose.

If he gave you faulty guidance, you have a potential case for breach of warranty. This may be difficult to prove, but the door is open for possible relief. If you select the gear independently or choose a specific brand or design you like, the warranty will not apply.

Implied warranties can be disclaimed by excluding them in writing. Another disclaimer is to use the term "as is" in a contract for sale, which effectively cancels any warranty or guarantee associated with that specific product. Consult your state law because certain products are exempt from such disclaimers.

Closely scrutinize and understand every detail of a warranty before you buy. If you purchase a product with the promise of "satisfaction guaranteed," what criteria will be used to determine whether the appropriate level of customer satisfaction is achieved? What must the business do to compensate the customer if the product is deemed unsatisfactory? Any company offering such a guarantee opens the door to all sorts of claims, some of which may be fraudulent. Always make sure you read the fine print.

If there's reasonable doubt about what a warranty covers, assume it's open to negotiation. If the terms of a warranty are not precise and subject to differing interpretations, those terms are open to negotiation. While there may be significant pressure for you to accept a determination or decision by the warrantor, you're not obligated to consent to it. Defend what you believe based on the facts as you know and understand them.

Buying and Selling a Car

Automobile buying has undergone dramatic changes since I was a child. In those days, most people bought cars from a dealer, whether new or used. There were independent used car lots here and there, along with private sale listings in the newspaper classified ads section. The ads listed a phone number for the owner, so you called the number and hoped someone answered because there were no answering machines if they didn't pick up. If you wanted that car, you had to keep calling and calling, sometimes for days if they were out of town, until you were lucky enough to make a connection.

We've come a long way since then. Craigslist is the first online resource I used to replace newspaper classifieds, and alternative methods for buyers and sellers have exploded in popularity. They emphasize convenience, speed, and minimum paperwork. I would only buy a car online if I saw and drove it first, but some might consider that old-fashioned. I don't buy groceries online because I'm picky about fresh meats, fruits, and vegetables.

Since I won't pretend to know how to advise anyone who buys a car online, I'll focus on the time-honored method of doing it in person at a dealership. My tips are directed toward the personal approach, but many apply equally well to your chosen purchase technique. So, if you plan to buy privately or through other means, I encourage utilizing as many of these tips as you can.

Arm yourself with as much information as possible about the cars you're interested in. The internet, auto magazines, *Consumer*

Reports, and the *Kelley Blue Book* are good sources, particularly if you're in the market for a used car. Find out if there are unadvertised dealer holdbacks and financial incentives that directly benefit the dealer. A holdback is a percentage of sales repaid to the dealer by the manufacturer. This repayment artificially raises the dealer's vehicle cost on paper and makes the vehicle appear more expensive than it actually is. That money belongs in your pocket, not the dealer's.

Bring your research to the dealer, including market values, current rebates, financing offers, and trade-in estimates. Consumer services, some charging a fee, can provide relevant cost data on specific car models. All it takes is an internet search to track down precisely what you're looking for. Given the elevated price ranges of new and used cars, it's worth your time and money to come prepared with the best information possible.

Preparation pays off in the long run and will show the salesman you know what you're talking about before the negotiation starts. Establishing your credibility right off the bat will put him on notice that you've got your act together.

You don't want to look like you have money to burn, so dress the part. Leave your bespoke Antonio Liverano suit in the closet. Dress casually but professionally to look like someone the sales-man will take seriously. If you're fortunate enough to wear a Patek Philippe, Breguet, or Vacheron Constantin watch, leave those at home along with any expensive jewelry. Whatever you do, don't arrive at the dealership in a Maybach S 680 or Porsche 911 GT3 RS unless you plan to trade it in. If you're perched above the fray in a lofty, high-income bracket, this is not the time to impress the salesman with your opulent lifestyle. If you appear to have gobs of disposable income to spare, the dealer will be more than willing to take it away from you. I definitely would.

One way to save money is to buy when dealers actively clear out their inventories at the end of a model year. Focus on when they make room for the new model shipments, which vary by manufacturer.

While you lose a year's depreciation by buying the current model, that's not a critical factor if you plan to keep the car for several years. Dealers also advertise special discounts on certain holidays and other times of the year when they score their inventory. If you can't plan your purchase during one of these times, keep pursuing similar discounts independently. Always bargain for unadvertised price reductions.

Dealers might ask if you have a budget or the maximum amount you plan to spend. Never answer that question directly. You should have a budget, but keep it to yourself. Your leverage to negotiate something lower than your budget disappears if you disclose it because the salesman now knows the amount you're willing to spend. Your objective is to get the best car that meets your needs while spending the least money to buy it. When asked if you have a budget, reply that what you'll pay depends on the car and the attractiveness of the overall deal. Be intentionally vague.

When looking at cars on the lot, don't show your cards by zeroing in on one car and showering it with all your attention and affection. If the salesman sees you're in love with that car and have to own it, get ready to pay a higher price. Take your time and look around a bit. If you see something you like, put on your poker face and talk about it with the salesman. Limit the discussion to the facts and keep any emotion out of it. The endgame you're playing is to eventually buy the car the salesman thought you liked the least.

If you lack confidence in your ability to deal independently, sometimes it helps to bring a friend along. In addition to providing moral support, you can break off and huddle with your friend. Use it as a diversionary tactic to stall, buy time, and strategize together. This approach also places you on a more equal footing if the salesman elects to involve the sales manager or other associates to try and break an impasse. As a general rule, the higher you go up their management chain, the more flexibility they'll have on price.

There's a very good reason why the sticker price (Manufacturer's Suggested Retail Price—MSRP) is displayed on cars. It gives the asking price an aura of authenticity and provides a healthy profit margin for the dealer. From your perspective, it's only a starting point for negotiations, and your singular goal is to chip away as much of that margin as possible. Don't be confused or fooled by the Dealer Invoice Price, which you're to believe is the number to shoot for as a target reduction from the MSRP. Don't fall for it. You never want to negotiate downward from an artificially high starting point. Please read that last sentence again because it's one of the oldest, most effective tricks in the book.

If you use any dealer quote as a baseline, start at the actual dealer cost and move up from there. When I was a second-classman at USAFA, about 300 of my classmates and I bought new Corvettes from Williams Chevrolet in Colorado Springs. We paid dealer cost plus $49, and all the options were two-thirds of the retail cost. With that many orders, we had tremendous leverage to shape our deal, and there was genuine competition among dealers to capture our business. The promotional opportunities that arise from that type of colossal sale are practically boundless, and Williams took full advantage of them.

Absent that kind of leverage, I'd be surprised if dealers disclosed their actual cost. It's none of your business unless they want to make it your business. If they refuse, tell them you're not willing to negotiate down from their proposed number either. Feel free to make an offer that's unrelated and independent from any number they've floated, regardless of the source.

Automobile options are to a car dealer what desserts and drinks are to a restaurant. These items have the biggest price markups on a percentage basis and are where they make their real money. If you walk into a restaurant and order a meal with a glass of water and nothing else, they'll take your money, but their profit margin will be relatively low. The same rationale applies to cars, so dealers will gladly pile on as many options as possible. They'll cost you far more than what it costs the dealer to add them.

Only buy the options you need and will use, and avoid service contracts and extended warranties. The ones to exclude are rustproofing, undercoating, fabric protection, and windshield etching. For the options you do want, include all of them as part of your first offer. You'll pay much more for them if you tack them on as you close in on a final deal. Most new cars are better quality than ever and come with excellent warranties as part of the purchase price, so there's no reason to invest in additional coverage.

Before making an offer, review your financial condition and determine how much car you can realistically afford. The issue of dealer financing will surface at some point in the process. Whether you go with that or set up your own is your call to make, but base it on accurate data you can use to calculate your total cost. The dealer financing terms, especially the interest rate and total loan runout cost, should be studied closely in a nonpressure environment and compared to what you can do on your own.

There are a variety of theories on how to deal with a potential trade-in vehicle. I prefer to sell mine privately because I can maximize my return. That can be a time-consuming process, and you may end up dealing with buyers who aren't serious, can't come up with the money, or will otherwise waste your time. Also, you might do better with a trade-in if you're buying a relatively expensive car since there's usually a direct correlation between trade-in value and the magnitude of your out-of-pocket expense.

If I go with the trade, I'll tell the salesman my purchase of a new car is contingent on accepting the trade-in as part of the deal, but we'll negotiate its value as a separate transaction. In other words, I won't negotiate a bottom-line price for the new car that includes an unidentified allowance for my trade-in. Since this approach differs from the one many people take, an explanation of the relative trade-offs between the two is in order. It's simply a combination of basic psychology and mathematics.

If you elect to do a bottom-line negotiation, there's a reasonable chance there will be one price for the new car that assumes the trade-in without disclosing the amount allowed for it. The salesman might say he'll sell you the new vehicle you want for $40,000 plus your trade-in. You don't know what he's allowing for the trade-in because you never agreed on a price for the new car without it. This approach enables him to entice you by reducing the cost of the new vehicle while taking that money back by undercutting the fair market value of your used one.

I prefer to do two negotiations rather than one by locking in the price of the new car first and then dealing separately with the trade-in as a standalone transaction. Now you've got leverage because if you can't get what you believe to be a fair price for your trade-in, you can always back out of the purchase because of the contingency you established going in. You can then opt to sell your car privately and renegotiate the purchase of the new one. The loss of a potential sale might motivate him to give you more for the trade-in. Dealers are always looking for good trade-ins because their mechanics will go through them to ensure they're running satisfactorily and thoroughly clean them for resale. It's a very profitable part of their business.

Salesmen expect you to challenge and bargain hard with them, so there's no reason to disappoint them. They also know there are many other dealers to choose from, and nothing stops you from shopping around. They don't want you walking away, so keep that in mind as you apply pressure to get an attractive deal. If you roll over too quickly, you've left money on the table that should be going home with you. Always remember you can walk away, that this provides you with the ultimate in leverage, that it's the dealer's greatest fear, and that you'll never get it for less than your first offer. The salesman may be in a hurry to finish, but you aren't. Patience is your best ally.

Here are a few final tips on closing a deal. Being prepared puts you in the strongest position possible. Use your experiences, instincts, and intuition to size up and understand the salesman you'll be working with. Capitalize on your strengths, exploit his weaknesses to the maximum extent possible, and take advantage of every leverage opportunity.

In a weak economy, salesmen still want to make their sales targets and don't want to let a serious customer go out the door without closing a deal. I once had the experience of a salesman making a final offer after I was already out the door and about to drive home. If you've done your homework and stay composed, you'll get the car you want at the price you want.

Selling your car privately puts you on the flip side of the tug-of-war of opposing forces. Selling it when you don't have to relieves the pressure to make a sale within an arbitrary time frame and increases your leverage dramatically. You gain the advantage of setting the anchor price wherever you want and holding it there for as long as you want. That's a luxury you don't want to give up.

Before you put it up for sale, take care of any routine maintenance and clean it thoroughly. If you prefer not to do it, take it to a professional detailer. There's an excellent chance you'll recover that cost when you sell the car. Buyers like a used car that runs well and looks good, so pay attention to the simple stuff.

Set your price knowing potential buyers will offer you less money. The only question is how much less. Base your first counteroffer on their offer. If it's significantly lower than your asking price, reduce your price only slightly when you counter, sending a message that their offer is not in the ballpark of how far you're willing to go. How much they move up on their counter is pivotal. If buyers get the message that they're much too low and still want the car, they'll kick their number up enough to show they want to stay in the game. If they don't move enough to satisfy you, move down slowly in small increments.

You can't get back what you give up in a counteroffer that's lower than it needs to be. Be patient and allow time to get a feel for where the buyer is headed. If you sense they're wasting your time, move on to the next one. There are plenty of buyers out there who are shopping for a car because they need one. If you don't need to sell, exploit their sense of urgency whether they show it or not.

Buying and Selling a House

--- --- --- --- --- --- --- --- --- --- --- --- --- --- --- --- --- ---

S ome tactics and strategies outlined in "Buying and Selling a Car" apply to many other purchases, including a house. I won't repeat those here, so I recommend you read that chapter before reading this one. It will serve as a jumping-off point for my tips that apply more to real estate but are not necessarily exclusive to that process.

When buying a house, the first three pieces of information most realtors want to know are: (1) location, (2) size (number of bedrooms, etc.), and (3) budget. There could be several more secondary questions to narrow your search. Responding to #1 and #2 is common sense and necessary to start looking. What should you do about #3? My answer is more complicated than handing over a number to the realtor.

As a buyer, I never disclose my budget for two reasons. First, keeping my budget a secret increases my leverage. Second, regarding the asking price, I want to consider more expensive houses than I can afford and view those that exceed my budget.

The first reason should be intuitively obvious. Very wealthy people rarely shop for big-ticket items themselves for an explicit motive. Let's illustrate with an example to demonstrate how obvious it is. Assume you own a house you believe is worth at least $500,000. If Warren Buffett submits an offer for $400,000, how much leverage does he have to drive the price down? You know he's worth billions, and that $100,000 is chump change to him. However, it's a different ballgame if Buffett submits an offer without disclosing his name

through an authorized agent or attorney with signature authority. He has far more leverage working through an intermediary
who effectively hides his enormous wealth. Consistent with this
approach, many wealthy people purchase homes through a trust,
limited liability company (LLC), or other legal entity to disguise
their ownership interest.

When Walt Disney was looking for land in Florida that would
become the site of Disney World, he wanted to avoid what had
happened in Anaheim, California, when the construction of Dis-
neyland became public knowledge. As developers swooped in to
buy properties near the proposed site, the value of land formerly
home to orange groves instantly skyrocketed. He intended to keep
his plans a secret and acquire a substantial acreage of land in the
Orlando area to protect the resort from encroachment.

Disney attorney Paul Helliwell acted as the point man. He
enlisted the cooperation of Billy Dial, the president of First National
Bank of Orlando, to assist him in negotiating with existing land-
owners. Publicly, land was acquired for a major industrial development, and the buyer's identity was kept secret. Dummy companies,
including the Reedy Creek Ranch Corporation, were established
as buyers, and local real estate agents were mobilized to make cash
offers on various tracts of land in the area, which helped to minimize the paper trail. Many owners were eager to unload what was
mostly swampland at bargain prices for the time. To Disney, this
was the perfect location to create the lakes and waterways central
to the park's appeal and recreational opportunities.

By maintaining secrecy, Disney bought 27,400 acres for about
$5 million, at an average cost of approximately $182 per acre. Once
Florida Governor Haydon Burns announced on 25 October 1965,
that Disney would develop a new park, real estate prices in the surrounding area soared to record heights, with land changing hands at
several thousand dollars per acre. Those escalating prices confirmed
why Disney didn't want to disclose that he was the buyer for the

vast acreage he purchased. If the sellers had known the identity of the actual buyer, Disney would have lost his leverage and paid far more for the land.

The second reason is a simple mathematical exercise with a dash of psychology thrown into the mix. Assume I'm prepared to pay around $500,000 for a house, and I've enlisted the help of a buyer's agent to make it happen. If I tell him my budget is $500,000, he'll produce listings pegged at that price or lower. That's not what I want to see. The only listings I'll consider are those that exceed $500,000. Why? Regardless of the asking price, I'll negotiate it down to what I can afford. If the first house doesn't work out as planned, it's on to the next one. I'm always setting the bar higher than where I expect to end up.

I realize this approach isn't always feasible. We've had periods called "seller's markets" when there were bidding wars and houses consistently sold well above the asking price. The idea of negotiating a better deal was off the table, and if you tried it, you weren't taken seriously as a potential buyer. The last time we experienced this phenomenon coincided with the COVID-19 pandemic. The Federal Reserve printed trillions of dollars out of thin air to goose the economy and kept interest rates at historic lows. A 30-year fixed mortgage averaged around 3% for much of this time, creating a golden opportunity for buyers who might otherwise not qualify for a loan to jump into the market. The result was predictable. Sellers could dictate prices virtually without resistance, causing them to skyrocket to their highest level in history.

What do you do when the seller has all the leverage? That depends on your circumstances, but if I don't have to buy at that time, I won't. When interest rates rise enough, that will eventually have the effect of reducing prices. However, there's always a trade-off in the mortgage payment since it's a function of both the price paid and the loan's interest rate. As one goes up, the other may go down, and vice versa.

Under normal market conditions that extraordinary monetary policies haven't distorted, you can negotiate the price because the seller has doubtless included a margin that he's willing to concede to a qualified buyer. Your intention is to take that margin away and more.

I won't disclose my budget if I'm working with a buyer's agent, but he needs something to work with. The agent won't waste time showing multimillion-dollar homes if there's no likelihood that I'd buy one. Give the agent a range based on the twin goals of buying a house listed above your budget without disclosing your bottom-line number. Keep that number to yourself no matter what. Your leverage is severely compromised if your number is inadvertently leaked to the seller.

If I'm prepared to pay $500,000, as previously indicated, I'll give the agent a price range of around $450,000 to $650,000. These are ballpark figures dependent on current market conditions in the specific areas where I'm looking. The agent can now compile listings within that range. Although I may not be able to afford a house at the high end of that range, I'm only using the listings to identify viable negotiation targets. I'm doing the negotiating, not the agent, so I'm the one devising the overall strategy for getting the house I want at the price I want.

Providing a price range instead of a firm budget will expand the volume of listings the agent has to deal with, making his job more complicated. However, I intend to look only at some of them. To sharpen the focus on properties of highest interest, I'd also provide relevant criteria to narrow the search, such as square footage, number of bedrooms and bathrooms, lot size, etc. Combining those criteria with my price range creates a flexible search profile that should be manageable for both of us.

Negotiating through real estate agents is a perfect solution for those who prefer to avoid confrontation. It becomes a battle of the forms as both parties make counteroffers with their latest price and conditions of sale. I've never had a face-to-face encounter in any of my real estate transactions. I've dealt exclusively with agents who carried the forms back and forth, which took time and increased the chances of something important falling through the cracks during the process. I prefer a different way of doing business. In an ideal world, I'd want the buyer and seller to sit in one room and negotiate the same way I would for any other personal or business-related contract. I can't read body language and test someone's resolve by trading forms in a sterile environment.

Since we're seemingly stuck with a system that circumvents face-to-face negotiations, there are some things we can do to maximize our position. Clearly and succinctly identify all conditions and contingencies with each successive offer. If the other party proposes conditions that are unacceptable to you, challenge them immediately. Never give the other party or agents the slightest hint of where you might be willing to settle or that you're even close to that number. Whenever you provide information you're not required to give them, you jeopardize your number one weapon: Leverage.

The bottom line is that disclosing your budget is a deathtrap, whether buying a house or any other significant purchase. That knowledge will be used against you by the other party, putting you at an immediate disadvantage. When making such a purchase, you'll be asked how much you plan to spend or what you can afford. It's none of their business, so don't answer the question directly. Instead, either decline to respond or give them a range based on the previous discussion. How you proceed depends upon the circumstances of your transaction and what you believe is in your best interest to achieve your goal.

Many of the same tactics and strategies can be used to buy and sell a house or car. However, timing is a paramount consideration when buying and selling real estate. When realtors talk about buyer's and seller's markets, they're referring to the supply and demand dynamic that's a function of current economic and financial conditions. These are my definitions for those terms.

- Buyer's market: When prices are lower due to economic downturn, oversupply of new homes for sale, high inventory of existing homes for sale, higher than average interest rates, declining stock market, declining consumer confidence, homeowners leaving the area you are buying in due to high crime rates, high taxes, unfavorable political climate, etc.

- Seller's market: When prices are higher due to Federal Reserve monetary policies, historically low interest rates, economic prosperity, bullish stock market, increasing consumer confidence, inadequate supply of homes for sale, and homebuyers flocking to a desirable area due to low crime rates, low taxes, favorable political climate, etc.

During the pandemic period of March 2020 through most of 2022, we experienced a strong seller's market caused by two primary factors: (1) historically low mortgage rates, and (2) low inventory of homes for sale. Cheap financing enabled buyers to purchase homes that would have otherwise been out of reach, and this demand drove prices much higher for over two years.

Stories abounded that multiple buyers offered more than the asking price, culminating in outright bidding wars. As a potential buyer, how can you possibly negotiate in that environment? If you offer less than the asking price, won't the seller take the offer (and you) as a joke? The answer, admittedly, is yes. Sometimes, the other party has insurmountable leverage because the supply/demand ratio is entirely out of equilibrium. The fact that all real estate is unique puts the buyer in a highly disadvantageous position under those conditions.

How you price your home is mainly dependent on the current market. Over the years, the biggest mistake I've observed is that sellers initially price the home too high in a weakening market. As the market continues to deteriorate, they keep lowering the price, and at some point, the listing gets stale and uninteresting to potential buyers. Successive price drops, known as "chasing the market," worsen the situation.

The solution is to avoid getting too greedy when setting the original asking price. In a buyer's market, set your price below the market and separate yourself from the competition. Give potential buyers a solid reason to check out your property first. You might get less than you wanted if you sell, but you'll avoid larger losses downstream if the market continues to decline for an extended period.

Tips, Tactics and Strategies

Negotiating is a pyramidal hierarchy that includes three layers or building blocks from top to bottom: (1) tactics, (2) strategies, and (3) principles. The foundation of the pyramid consists of the fundamental principles previously outlined in this book.

- Ask for what you want, not what you think you can get
- You'll never get it for less than your first offer
- Unless you have a compelling reason not to, always make a counteroffer
- Never negotiate against yourself
- Use every scrap of leverage you have, and pound it home like there's no tomorrow
- "Compromise" doesn't mean I'll meet you halfway
- Always be prepared to walk away, and not necessarily as a last resort
- Make the other party earn and pay for every concession you make
- Only negotiate with someone empowered to commit
- Negotiate on friendly turf whenever possible
- Everything is always on sale, until it isn't
- Beware of the warranty trap

Start every negotiation by relying on these principles as the foundation for your negotiating plan. The next step is to develop an overall strategy that implements the principles. As the negotiation progresses, you create and implement tactics designed to execute your strategy. Tactics are individual actions targeted toward specific objectives. For example, figuring out subsequent counteroffers is a tactical move that will be different each time you make such a move.

This book discusses how to approach various conditions and circumstances you're likely to encounter, and I've provided details on tactics to consider utilizing. Remember that negotiations are dynamic, and you'll often feel like you're aiming at a moving target. Be prepared to change course quickly and efficiently to maintain your tactical advantage.

All other things being equal, the seller has the upper hand at the beginning of most negotiations because he can establish the initial parameters, including the asking price. Unless he's desperate to sell, he can also control the pace and who's allowed to participate in the talks. The seller has significant leverage that may be difficult to overcome without a potent strategy to take the offensive and knock it down. The seller must prepare for that offensive and take specific actions to preserve his advantage.

You have options when establishing your asking price. One is to set a fixed, take-it-or-leave-it price from which you won't negotiate. That approach is common since almost every U.S. retailer does that. There's a price tag on each item in the store, and you either pay that price or leave without the item. Some retailers will negotiate on higher-cost items, but they typically don't publicize that fact. Most retailers sell new, unused goods, which they pay wholesale prices to acquire. They add labor and overhead costs to the wholesale amount before adding profit. Realistically, the profit is the only part of the total price they can negotiate.

A private seller of used goods has fewer constraints than a retailer that has to cover its costs. You have the flexibility and latitude to ask for whatever you want, even if it means taking a loss. If you've gotten many years of use out of an old car you're ready to sell, you know you'll take a depreciation loss unless it's achieved collectible status. The flip side usually applies to real estate, which has historically risen in value and could net you a profit upon resale. All of this depends on the prevailing economic climate.

Setting your asking price depends highly on what you're selling. For example, if I have an oil painting by a little-known artist, the historical record of that artist's sales may be minimal. That gives me more flexibility in pricing it, but buyers will be wary of paying too much for an artist without a proven track record. Contrast this type of sale with that of a used automobile. Tons of pricing data are available to guide you on both sides of the negotiation.

I follow general rules for sellers while maintaining the flexibility to modify and adapt them to the unique circumstances of each negotiation.

First, establish a reasonable asking price with sufficient maneuvering room to negotiate downward. How much margin should you add to the price where you ultimately want to settle? There's no fixed percentage that I use across the board. The margin amount primarily depends on what I'm selling, competitive pressures, supply and demand conditions, and the current economic environment. Once you factor in all the variables you believe will affect the price, it's a judgment call. Ask yourself; is it a buyer's or seller's market?

Second, present the asking price as a complement to value and benefits. Your primary focus should be on the item and not its price tag. If necessary, explain how it works and how flawlessly it works. Do some salesmanship without being overbearing. While he's a tough act to follow, try channeling the great Billy Mays.

Third, don't talk as if there's any room for negotiation. Don't say, "I'd like to get something close to $200 for it." That statement is begging me to offer less, assuredly a lot less. You might as well have said, "If I'm lucky, some sucker will pay me $50 for it." Present your asking price with total confidence, as though you just poured concrete around it, making it an immovable object. You don't say that, but that's the impression you want the buyer to have. You'd be surprised at how well and how often that works, resulting in a quick sale at your price.

Fourth, be prepared to deal with objections and counteroffers if you don't get a quick sale. Have a plan of attack mapped out that preserves as much of your margin as possible while still completing the sale.

Fifth, be ready to trade something in exchange for a lower price. For example, if the buyer insists on 20% off, you might consider that option if he doubles the quantity purchased or extends the delivery schedule by several months. Keep all your cards on the table and offer ways to make the deal acceptable to both sides.

Sixth, generate a list of concessions that cost you little at the bottom line and don't endanger your strategy. Each one represents a potential deduction from your margin. Peel them off as needed and take credit for them when you counteroffer. Make the point that you're doing this to bring closure to the negotiation.

My most challenging negotiations involved buying critical parts and materials from a sole-source vendor. Your leverage is practically nonexistent when you desperately need a product that only one company makes. If you're lucky, their supply exceeds demand, and you might be able to weasel a deal here and there, but don't count on it. If I'm the seller of such a product, the sticker price is the sale price. Period.

Yard sales are a common occurrence across the country. Local ordinances dictate how and when they occur, but most places have similar rules. People expect to pay rock-bottom prices at such sales, but your idea of rock bottom may differ from mine.

Buyers are in control because people hold such sales to eliminate unused stuff clogging up storage closets, attics, and garages. I will only pay less than I'd be willing to pay. If I'm the seller, I know

I'm not in control. I didn't haul all that junk outside, intending to move it back inside at the end of the day. That doesn't mean I'll give it away unless you're a charity. So, I'll talk up what I'm selling, but prepare to take less than I'd like.

Beware of negotiation tricks designed to throw you off your game, add confusion to the process, and possibly cause you to commit an unforced error. The question is, do tricks really work? The answer is sometimes, but a simple rule applies to the negotiations I've done. There's an inverse relationship between the likelihood tricks will work and the experience level of your opponent. So, employing tricks on a competent negotiator will probably fall flat and make you look foolish. Tricks might work on someone who doesn't know what they're doing, but don't bet on it.

Here's one example. If my car is for sale with an asking price of $18,000, and you make an offer of $15,177, am I supposed to believe there's science and mathematics behind that number because it's so precise? Nice try, but I'm not going to fall for that trick. There's no difference between that number and $15,000. Adding the extra $177 doesn't give it more authenticity than if you had rounded it off. You don't have detailed calculations to back it up, so why bother? However, some fall for it and attach unearned credibility to an offer containing five significant digits. The reverse case won't work on me either. Asking $299 for your old canoe won't entice me to buy it any more than $300 would.

One trick I've encountered several times is the last-minute discount. Pretend you're the seller, you've negotiated a deal with the buyer, and you're ready to sign the contract. Before signing, the buyer tells you the deal is off unless the agreed price is reduced by 10%. He tells you this directive came straight from the company president and is a take-it-or-leave-it offer.

Walk away. If it's a bluff, you'll get called back, and you can sign or not. If it's not a bluff, you refuse to do business again with a company that won't stand behind its agreements.

There's no shortage of books available that provide a variety of so-called tricks to enhance your negotiating game. Stay away from anything that looks too simple and too good to be true because they usually aren't what they appear to be. If you're the target of such tricks, shoot them down immediately with logic and common sense. These are your two best weapons against those who'll waste your time with amateur schemes.

Some of the unconventional tactics listed below might qualify as borderline trickery, but I wouldn't include them if they hadn't worked for me.

- **Go Alone**
- **No Nothing**
- **Chirping Crickets**
- **Backflip Bombshell**
- **Key Question**
- **Escape Hatch**
- **Trap Door**
- **Black Hole**

"Go Alone" is an atypical tactic that plays upon the other party's expectations and what I know they'll assume based on experience. In most of the business negotiations I've done, the companies on each side fielded a team that included three to five people from the following disciplines: program management, business and finance, contracts, pricing, and engineering. The engineering representative would rotate in and out depending on the specific section of the proposal under review. That group typically included design, mechanical, structural, electrical, and systems integration and testing.

On the first day of negotiations, the opposing team would arrive with binders full of proposal data and information about whatever we were negotiating. Most of the materials would never be used, but they believed the piles of paper would intimidate us into thinking they were prepared to deal with any issue that arose and baffle us if necessary.

It would be easy for me to bring even more binders than they did to outdo them at their own game. Instead, I would do just the opposite. I'd arrive at the first meeting alone or with one other member of my team, armed with nothing more than business cards. No binders, notebooks, phones, computers, notepads, or pens appeared anywhere in sight. "No Nothing." This disturbing scene would provoke a swift inquiry as to why we were unprepared to negotiate and why our team was missing. I'd explain they weren't required to get things rolling, and I was prepared to dive right in without further delay. The real fun would begin once they got over their disbelief and bewilderment.

Who was more intimidated by this scene? Were we intimidated by the presence of all their people and their mountains of data? Or were they intimidated by only one or two people from our team with nothing to see besides the clothes on our backs? From the looks on their faces, it was always clear that this was a first for them, and they were wondering—Who are these guys, anyway?

With few exceptions, I've found that bringing mountains of data is more akin to a security blanket than a true asset. If I'm on the other side of the table, you're not intimidating me, and I wonder why you bothered to strain yourselves by lugging all that weight to every session. I view it more as a bluff than anything else, but a successful bluff requires far more than reams of paper. I've used the No Nothing approach sparingly and only when it was apparent that the other party intended to spook us with a sizable team and swamp us with irrelevant data.

If you could get inside my head, you'd discover I'd do almost anything to throw the other side off their game, upset the status quo, and make them wonder why they brought five nonessential people to the table. Any more profound or byzantine psychological impacts were icing on the cake.

While my preference is to negotiate in person, occasionally circumstances dictate otherwise. Telephone negotiations offer the chance to use a few tactics that are more effective when you can't see the other party. My clear favorite is dead silence, or "Chirping Crickets." When the other party says something with the expectation of a reply, I'll say nothing. Dead air can be rattling and unsettling. It leaves the other person wondering if you heard what they said and if you understood it. If so, why you didn't respond? You've left them hanging, and that's precisely where they don't want to be.

Predictably, they'll start talking again to fill the dead air and provide further explanations and insights into what they were saying. They're hoping this will prompt some sign of life at your end. Sometimes, this becomes a goldmine of information they voluntarily hand over without you saying a word. The less you talk, the more they talk. It's a thing of beauty when it happens.

I've rarely used the "Backflip Bombshell" over the years. It's so rare that it's been over a decade since I last dropped this bomb. The easiest way to describe this tactic is to tell you about the first time I used it in a sizable negotiation. Our team had submitted a proposal for a state-of-the-art spacecraft payload to our customer. In round numbers, our bid totaled $50 million. The potential for additional follow-on work was extremely high, so our proposal was very tight and included no margin to give away in negotiations. Our company wanted the contract, and we submitted a bare-bones proposal to maximize our odds of winning. We expected to negotiate a number that was very close to our bid. Otherwise, we knew that a cost overrun was almost a certainty.

Formal negotiations commenced with a comprehensive review of the terms and conditions that would apply to the contract. It was evident that the customer had thoroughly reviewed our proposal, performing a technical and cost analysis to establish their initial position. This process was routine. I knew our bid was tight, so I was utterly unprepared for their first offer: $35 million, a 30% reduction to our proposal. Our team was in a total state of shock. We knew completing the work for $50 million would be tough, so cutting $15 million from that was unacceptable. Either they were joking or made a monumental mistake during their proposal evaluation. Or, they were testing us to see how we'd react, something I'm inclined to do occasionally.

Well, we didn't react. I called for an immediate recess and huddled in a separate room with our team. Then, we retaliated among ourselves. After getting past the expletives and asking ourselves if these people had gone mad, we discussed how their absurd offer might alter our strategy. We all agreed we had to send them a powerful message while remembering we wanted this contract. We knew other bidders were out there but also knew we were in the best position to produce the revolutionary hardware they wanted. There was no payoff in attacking them for their ridiculous offer, so we decided to make a counteroffer that would send the message for us: $55 million, an increase of $5 million to our original proposal. Bombs away! Kaboom!! The gap between our positions immediately jumped from $15 million to $20 million. Welcome to my world!

A move like this contradicts the traditional negotiating stereotype, so I must stop here and make an important point. While counteroffers are normally intended to close the gap between positions, nothing stops you from going in the opposite direction. Doing the unexpected gets my adrenaline pumping because I know the other party will come unglued and unhinged when I blow up their strategy.

We reconvened in the conference room, and I presented our counteroffer of $55 million. I explained that further review of our proposal confirmed the inadvertent exclusion of several critical elements from our original submission, and we were now including those in our updated proposal. What we didn't disclose was that we had scrubbed some tasks out to cut our bid to a rock-bottom number, and we were restoring them to jack it back up. Without saying it explicitly, we sent a message that they had insulted us with an offer they knew was unreasonably low. We didn't appreciate how they wasted our valuable time entertaining such offers.

Our counteroffer raising our proposal by $5 million was the equivalent of Muhammad Ali's devastating right-hand blow that knocked Joe Frazier's mouth guard to the mat in the thirteenth round of the "Thrilla in Manila." Well, it wasn't quite that dramatic, but we got their attention in a very big way.

After hearing our counteroffer, the opposing party alternately ranted, panted, and chanted for several minutes as they accused us of negotiating in bad faith and not negotiating at all. "You're going in the wrong direction!" they squealed. "How can we ever settle if you keep adding money to your proposal?" they shrieked. We sat there patiently and listened until they ran out of steam. I then told them we'd be pleased to entertain their counteroffer. They didn't walk away, and our plan was successfully executed.

Now, the ball was in their court. If they thought we would roll over and play their silly split-the-difference game, they just got a rude awakening to reality. Their next offer was $45 million, and we settled at $49 million, $1 million less than our original proposal. To this day, I believe they moved quickly to settle because they were afraid we'd find more things omitted from our proposal and keep bumping up our number. There's also no doubt in my mind that they knew their first offer was obscenely low, and they had to clear the wreckage to keep the negotiation from completely falling apart.

Knocking a million off our initial proposal was acceptable because we had to afford them a token of good faith to show their management they'd accomplished something. It was a small price to capture an important contract that would generate millions in profits from successive follow-on programs.

One last point. If we hadn't raised our offer to $55 million, there's no way we would have settled at $49 million. That additional $5 million gave us wiggle room we never would have had and allowed us to get back to where we wanted to be all along. The Backflip Bombshell had worked to perfection.

I always look for a "Key Question," preferably one pivotal and decisive question that will throw the other side for a loop and turn things upside down. Ideally, it will embarrass the other party and force them to radically change their negotiating posture and position. Identifying such a question works to my advantage consistently in a significant way.

An illustrative example of my methodology appears in the chapter titled "What's It Worth." I'd received an estimate to install vinyl siding on my house, and the fixed price seemed excessively high, so I asked the contractor a simple question: How many square feet of siding comprise your total cost estimate, and how did you calculate the number? By the time he figured out the answer, his proposal had dropped approximately 50% because of severe flaws in his original estimating methodology. That question alone obliterated his entire proposal and compelled him to start over and resubmit his estimate. A negotiator's best friend, leverage, was now in my court, and our contract was drastically reduced as a result.

I've found substantial flaws in cost proposals that saved me a ton of money, personally and professionally. The lessons learned are never to take anything at face value, assume nothing, read the fine print, and always challenge the boilerplate. Just because a seller hands you a five-page "standard contract that we always use" to sign doesn't mean you have to accept it. Everything, including the fine print, is open to modification or deletion. If the other party refuses to alter or delete onerous terms and conditions, take your business elsewhere. Only assent to a price after agreeing to all the terms and conditions of the sale.

Don't shake hands on a number that you find out later was based on incomplete data or flawed assumptions. The price should be the last thing you discuss whenever possible. Only conclude a negotiation when there's a meeting of the minds that includes a written, signed, and dated summary of everything agreed to. It will form the basis of any resulting contract.

"Escape Hatch" is a tactic I reserve strictly for business negotiations. It means the top executive of a company should rarely, if ever, negotiate on its behalf. This executive could be the CEO, president, or whatever comparable manager occupies the number one position in the decision-making hierarchy.

A company should always have at least one management level above the people in the room negotiating. Those people must have the power and authority to negotiate and commit the company to an agreement. I want that level above them in case they get stuck and need help to finish the negotiation.

If the CEO is in the room when the process deadlocks, there's no opportunity to change direction or rethink the strategy by appealing to a higher authority. The Escape Hatch allows the negotiating team to gracefully bring the discussions to a temporary halt, thereby allowing them to meet with the CEO for further guidance and direction. It provides one last chance to brainstorm and determine if there's a way to achieve closure that no one has thought of before. The CEO can act as a neutral overseer of the discussion, and it never hurts to engage a fresh set of eyes and ears with a novel perspective. While not an independent third party, the CEO should assume that role and guide the team to a position where they can hopefully find a way to cut a deal.

The top dog should stay away from the guts of the negotiation process unless intervention becomes necessary. He should remain on the bench and only come on the field in the fourth quarter when the game is on the line, the offense has stalled, and nothing else has worked. He's getting paid the big bucks to help push the ball over the goal line.

There's no escape hatch in my personal negotiations because I'm it. With no one else to appeal to, it's incumbent on me to avoid boxing myself into a corner that's difficult to escape from without substantially weakening my position. While walking away from a negotiation is often a superb tactical move, it's only effective if you execute it from a position of strength. If you do it in a debilitated condition, it's a flashing beacon of despair and desperation. Keep all your options open for as long as possible, and don't resort to concessions tempted by unyielding pressure and distress. You possess the power, you're in control, and you have no reason to relinquish either, no matter how tough the battle.

A prized tactic is the "Trap Door," where you lure the other side into asserting something you know is incorrect. While creating a scenario that entices them to take the bait, you open the trap door and watch them plunge straight through it. If you can set this up to occur during the early stages of the negotiation, it slaps a big question mark on the credibility of everything they say from that point forward.

In the example previously cited regarding the siding proposal, the Key Question simultaneously set up the Trap Door. To do this, I had to know the answer to the question before I asked it. Otherwise, you can't set the trap because the answer might surprise and work against you. In my case, I already knew the square footage estimate for the siding was about double what it should have been.

At that point, the trap was set. All I needed to pull the trap door was for the contractor to confess that he'd screwed up his estimate by using a seriously flawed aerial survey, and that's what happened. The survey was now a dead duck at the bottom of the trap chute, totally erased by a simple, straightforward analysis that only took a few minutes.

What could a "Black Hole" possibly have to do with negotiating? I stated earlier that negotiation is an art, not a science, but a temporary diversion into the dynamics of outer space enfolds just enough science to explain the connection. It helps to conceptualize a black hole in terms that, hopefully, we can all relate to.

This astronomical phenomenon generates a gravitational pull so powerful that nothing can escape it. Light, which travels at the speed limit of the universe, can't escape it. The surface or event horizon represents the outer ring or boundary of a black hole beyond which escape velocity would have to exceed the speed of light. Albert Einstein theorized that nothing can travel faster than light, so the event horizon is the point of no return where nothing would be visible to an outside observer attempting to look in.

Any particle or object approaching the speed of light would expand its mass exponentially and require an infinite energy supply to accelerate it. The black hole's mass is concentrated at the center, with infinite density. Escaping that mass is impossible based on current scientific theory.

Now, back to the negotiating table. The last place you want to find yourself in a negotiation is at the center of a black hole with no way out. The solution is to prevent yourself from getting sucked in to begin with. How? Here are a few tips.

- If you don't know the answer to a question, don't guess because it will come back to bite and haunt you in a huge way you can't recover from. "I don't know" or "I'll get back to you on that" is a perfectly acceptable answer, even if you never get back to them. There's a chance they'll forget about it and let it slide. If they do remember, be prepared with a rehearsed and hopefully bulletproof answer.

- On the flip side, do your best to know the answers to your questions before you ask them. Pretend you're going to trial even though you're not. It's borderline deadly to ask a question that blows up your entire negotiation strategy. Avoid asking a risky question if you don't already know the answer.

- Avoid unforced errors. If you're in a business negotiation with multiple team members who are inexperienced negotiators, I guarantee that one of them will say something that will make your head explode. Such mishaps commonly occur when experts on a specific subject attempt to refute challenges to your cost proposal. Many such experts won't know what to expect when their work is systematically dissected and chopped up by the other party. If you bring a rocket scientist into the room to bolster your cost estimate for a new rocket, verify that he's been coached and educated about the rules of engagement, especially when and when not to talk.

- Always answer the question asked, and no more. The human impulse is to shower the questioner with information that impresses him, going well beyond what's needed to answer the specific question. Suppress that urge to dazzle and impress the other party. Flaunting your remarkable wizardry will only open the door for new questions he hadn't thought of and will do nothing to dissuade him from probing even deeper into whatever valuable knowledge you may be trying to protect.

- It's commonplace for people to make up stuff during negotiations. They'll toss out numbers and statistics, reference polling data, cite experts, and draw conclusions as if they're cast in concrete and must be accepted as factual to prove their point. Whenever anyone does this to me, I ask to see their statistics and polls and tell them I want to talk to their experts. Nine times out of ten, the statistics don't exist, and their experts aren't available. Poll results are routinely cited in the news, but you rarely see the questions used to conduct the poll and collect the data. Experience reveals that a question's wording and how it's asked will skew the answers toward those sought by the pollster.

- Don't immerse yourself in the details to a degree where you miss the giant freight train barreling straight at you.

Unintended blindness to the big picture is the easiest way I know of to get sucked directly into the black hole, and it happens all the time. Always step back and assess where you are relative to your overarching objectives. Periodically do a top-down reality check of your effectiveness toward achieving those objectives. I understand the devil is in the details, and I don't dispute their relevance in a negotiation. However, if you consistently apply all your focus to the nitty gritty and never assuredly rise above it, the other party will run right over you and your trove of tidbits. In the end, the big picture rules.

Recurring Negotiations

Regularly negotiating with the same people and companies is commonplace in business. Threatening and pounding them into submission during your first negotiation will not bode well for future negotiations. There may never be another negotiation if they find you so offensive that they look elsewhere to buy whatever you're selling. Skilled negotiators thread the needle between negotiating aggressively and being too overbearing and obnoxious.

Operating a successful business requires the ability to negotiate effectively. Everything you buy and sell is negotiable, including rent, office supplies, products, maintenance costs, and employee salaries and benefits. Don't be reluctant to negotiate because you fear being branded as cheap or uncooperative. Avoiding confrontation and taking the path of least resistance is the equivalent of lighting a match to your hard-earned money. Show some backbone, dive in headfirst to protect your wealth, and share it only to the extent that's prudent, necessary, and makes good business sense.

Recurring negotiations offer an opportunity to build business relationships among the participants that can be very rewarding over the long run. You earn respect, and gaining the respect of the opposition works both ways. Your reputation will precede you in future negotiations, so it's beneficial to empathize with the other party, understand where they're coming from, and why they take certain unaligned positions. These practices will help you figure out what you can do to move them in your direction.

Always display rock-solid integrity, stand by your convictions, and engage in fair dealing on all matters. It also pays to have a sense of humor at the appropriate times.

Recognizing that both parties will set precedents during the first few encounters is crucial. I can't overstate how critical it is to preclude bad precedents that will come back to haunt you in the future. When you agree to something that the other side views as favorable to them, they'll expect the same accommodation in every subsequent negotiation. Moreover, they'll want something else to compensate for their perceived loss if they don't get it.

For example, if you manufacture wooden chairs and agree to produce ten in one month, you've set the bar for production time. If the same buyer returns six months later and wants another ten identical chairs, you can assume they'll expect them within the next month. You may have a hundred valid reasons why you can't duplicate that first-order performance, but once you set the bar, it's awkward and thorny to retreat from your original build schedule. If you're lucky, you'll still get the order, but you don't want to rely on luck.

One solution is to build slack into the first schedule you propose to give yourself extra time for unforeseen contingencies. Repeating that schedule on the next order will be much easier if you do that upfront. In the words of Marcus Tullius Cicero (106 BC–43 BC), "Men think they may justly do that for which they have a precedent."

Take advantage of the benefits of recurring negotiations and trade on them for as long as possible. Their value tends to fade over time because the other party is regularly figuring out ways to exploit whatever advantages they have against you. It certainly works both ways.

Negotiators develop habits and patterns of behavior that forecast how they'll react and what they'll do in response to your moves. Study their behavior and make mental notes for future reference. Use this information when constructing responses to their offers and counteroffers. A series of negotiations will also expose their strengths and weaknesses that might otherwise go undetected in a onetime encounter. Incorporate these data into your intelligence assessment of who you're facing and how they'll likely engage you.

The most effective negotiators know their business and don't let personalities and irrational behavior interfere with their mission. They keep their eye on the big picture and project a high degree of professionalism while simultaneously protecting their interests. You always want the other party to believe they got the best deal possible.

Professional relationships are a critical aspect of running any business. Negotiations sometimes conclude with a binding contract that requires performance by both parties. Maximum performance follows if all parties work together effectively and maintain a positive approach to continuing interactions while executing the contract provisions.

In the long run, it doesn't pay off to extract the last pound of flesh from the other party to secure a lopsided deal. The ripple effect of a snakebitten negotiation can produce intractable, long-term consequences. While heated confrontation is sometimes unavoidable in a high-stakes encounter, cooler heads must prevail at some point, and collaboration becomes the day's order. Otherwise, the risk is that nothing productive will happen, and any future business together may be off the table. You have the power to ensure that doesn't happen. Be prepared and be patient. Above all, never compromise your integrity and authenticity. You can be tough as nails without being a jackass.

Your reputation will precede you in the business world, and you want it to be sensible and solid. Being recognized as a tough negotiator is a positive as long as you're known to be forthright and evenhanded. Oil baron J. Paul Getty, Sr. clearly stated the bigger precept when he said, "You must never try to make all the money that's in a deal. Let the other fellow make some money, too, because if you have a reputation for always making all the money, you won't have many deals." Point made.

What Not To Do

— — — — — — — — — — — — — — — — — —

F ledgling negotiators often say and do things during a negotiation without comprehending the unintended consequences. One of the main reasons this happens is that it's difficult to ascertain and measure the psychological impact of what's said and done in real time. Experienced negotiators always look for clues to guide their strategy and tactics as they advance. Sometimes, they're subtle, and sometimes they explode right in your face. Either way, they can be an invaluable addition to your arsenal.

If you're interested in buying something with no asking price, never ask what they'll take for it. You're inviting them to quote a number much higher than what it's worth to you, and by default, that number becomes the anchor. Equally flawed is asking if they'll take a specific number from you. You've made it easy for them to say no because you've given them an out. If they don't want to take your number, they can ignore it and be less likely to make a counteroffer.

Another variation of this mistake is to suggest that someone toss out a number. This idea is worse than asking what they'll take because it implies that random numbers will be seriously considered. Don't give them a psychological advantage by creating the impression that the price requires no basis. Whether it does or not isn't the issue. You want the other party to believe their number must be derived from a substantive market value analysis.

Make an offer well below what you're willing to pay and see what happens. In this situation, there's an advantage to letting the other party set the anchor only if you have reason to believe they'll start much lower than you would. That reason must be rock-solid and bulletproof. My going-in position is to take control and drive the negotiation in my chosen direction.

If you're on the receiving end of an offer you consider ridiculous, you have several options. While you could say it's ridiculous, I recommend you not tell them that, at least not verbally. Instead, make the same point by responding with an equally absurd counteroffer. It sends the same message without saying a word. Then, sit back and wait to see what they do next. You could also ask them for a more realistic number, which puts them in the position of making two consecutive offers and negotiating against themselves. Just because you're never going to do that doesn't mean you can't encourage them to do it.

Accusing the other party of making a ridiculous offer may be offensive and sends a message that you don't trust them to be reasonable from a negotiation standpoint. It's fine if you believe that, but I wouldn't say it. Remember, you're trying to get a deal, and throwing around insulting accusations isn't a wise place to start. Psychology plays a critical role in every negotiation, and their perception of you in a positive light is indispensable. Don't rock the boat unnecessarily by saying something that might tune them out and turn them off. That accomplishes nothing except motivating them to dig their heels in even further.

You could also walk away or terminate the negotiation. Walking away can be temporary or permanent depending on what you say, if anything, on your way out the door. I cover this fundamental principle in detail in the section titled "Always be prepared to walk away, and not necessarily as a last resort." I permanently terminated a negotiation on just one occasion for a variety of reasons that piled on top of each other until I had no choice. Otherwise, it's always been tactical when I walked away with full intentions to resume negotiations in the future.

Unless I have a sound reason for altering my approach, my default condition is to deal with ridiculous offers by making counteroffers that clearly signal their number is way off the mark. They might not like my number, but I haven't said anything that detracts from their integrity and desire to reach a deal.

Never offer a range of prices. If you tell me you want between $100 and $150 for a baseball card, why would I pay $150 for it? It's nonsensical to offer a range like that. If you gave me that price range, I'd offer $50 because you've already confirmed you have no conviction regarding the card's worth. Anything over $100 is an absurd price to pay in this example. Whether you're the buyer or seller, always deal in one number and one number only.

Stay away from statements or indications that you believe the two parties are getting close to resolving differences. While asserting such a premature conclusion is tempting, it reduces your leverage by implying you're prepared to keep moving in their direction with subsequent offers. I don't telegraph anything to the other party about where we are in the process because I want to maintain my ability to keep undercutting their positions. I'd much rather have them lose all hope of getting what they want than give them hope that they might get it sooner rather than later.

To expedite closure when the opposing positions are relatively close, one party might offer to evenly split the remaining difference in price. I never propose a split because I want the option to refuse it. Proposing a split is a sign of weakness that spawns a loss of leverage. I'll do almost anything to hold onto whatever leverage I've got for as long as I can, even if it elevates the risk of delaying or complicating what appears to be an imminent settlement. If there's a split on the horizon, the other party has to put it on the table.

To illustrate the point, let's assume one party is at $10,000, and the other is at $12,000, and both sides are dug in with their respective positions. To close the gap, it's not uncommon to split the $2,000 delta and call it a day at $11,000. But if I'm the buyer at

$10,000 and propose a split at $11,000, what do I do if the seller says no? I've just told the seller I'm willing to move to at least $11,000, so it's not unreasonable for them to believe I might go even higher. Realistically, I've given up any chance of getting it for less than $11,000 regardless of what happens after that.

If the other side wants to close the final gap by splitting, stick the burden on them to propose it. Once a number is out there, you can't take it back, so put the other party in a position where that number comes from them. Never underestimate the power of psychological advantage. The way to maintain that advantage is to force the other party to show their hand first.

You'll forfeit leverage by showing desperation or acting in a manner that implies it. You can be sure the other party will pick up on it no matter how hard you try to disguise it. Any sense that you're pressed for time or making unnecessary concessions is like throwing fresh chum to a school of hungry sharks. They're not going to accommodate your situation or feel sorry for you. If I'm the other party, it will only motivate me to push even harder for a deal I might not otherwise get. Don't look, sound, or act desperately at any time in a negotiation. Masquerade, if necessary, put on your most convincing act, and keep doing whatever it takes to get the best deal possible.

Don't make statements you can't back up unless it's an intentional bluff, a topic I cover in detail in the chapter titled "Psychology 101." I'll consider bluffing if I've run out of bright ideas and my only viable option is walking away. Even then, I won't bluff unless I'm sure it's one that's very difficult to challenge with facts. Here's a simple example of a stupid bluff. You're selling what you claim is a rare model of an antique automobile, and only 20 like it are known to exist. Given the records currently available, that claim is easy to verify. If you're counting on the other party to accept your claim and move forward with the negotiation, you've set yourself up for disaster when they find out it's 200, not 20.

Several years ago, a retired employee sued the company we worked for under the whistleblower statute. The irony is that he was suing for financial misconduct that occurred under his watch as the proposal manager for the manufacturing effort on the contract at issue. He had signed and submitted bids to the customer that he later claimed were overbid because of the methodology used to back up his proposal. He alleged the government was overcharged through fraudulent billings, even though he knew there was a problem and could have corrected the bids before submission. No one else up the chain of command knew there were bidding errors or discrepancies before or during negotiations.

The bottom line is that he sued the company for something he consciously did while an employee. I couldn't believe this was possible, and my first reaction was that the company should countersue him for approving bidding estimates that he knew were false. That never happened.

The qui tam provisions of the False Claims Act allow whistleblowers to bring legal actions on behalf of the federal government. They'll typically collect 15% to 30% of the total monetary award if successful. The term "qui tam" is an abbreviated version of the Latin phrase, "qui tam pro domino rege quam pro se ipso in hac parte sequitur." Loosely translated, it means that he who sues on behalf of the king does the same for himself. For the record, I don't qualify as an amateur in the Latin language, but that translation should be close enough for government work.

Like most large companies, we had our in-house legal staff, but what I quickly discovered is they're what I refer to as "book lawyers." They don't step foot in a courtroom to litigate cases as trial attorneys. The company brings in outside legal counsel who specialize in litigation to defend itself. In this case, we retained a high-powered firm with specific expertise in qui tam actions. The whistleblower's lawyer referred to them as our "hired guns."

I don't think I'd be going too far out on a limb if I said most people take it for granted that professionals such as attorneys and accountants have the requisite skills to advise and represent them. That representation might include negotiating to resolve legal and tax issues requiring their assistance. That could be a huge mistake. Just because you have a great lawyer, never assume he's a great negotiator, a good negotiator, or even a mediocre negotiator. He could be a lousy negotiator who's counting on you to unknowingly presume otherwise. Unfortunately, too many people entrust life-altering negotiations such as divorce settlements, child custody disputes, and enormous business deals to lawyers who lack the skills to protect their clients' interests. Expert legal advice doesn't necessarily translate to superior negotiation results.

During the whistleblower lawsuit, I became intimately involved as part of the defense team because of my knowledge of the contract under assault. I worked closely with the lawyers during the discovery process and was present for every deposition. I knew I'd be called as a key witness if the case went to trial.

Our lawyers were impressive, but their weakest link was their inadequacy as negotiators. I surmised they may have attended a class or two in negotiating while attending law school or as part of their mandatory continuing education requirements. However, attending school won't teach you how to be a negotiator unless it's the school of hard knocks. You don't want your lawyer to undergo on-the-job training while attempting to negotiate your divorce settlement. It's too late to do you any good, may cause irreparable harm, and could cost you a lot of money.

Before the case went to trial, the parties reached a settlement that made the whistleblower wealthy. I couldn't get over the fact that this guy had knowingly submitted fallacious cost estimates, and now he was profiting handsomely from his misdeeds. The total settlement cost to our company included a gargantuan check to the government, a mammoth bill from our hired guns, a boatload of cash to the whistleblower, and a fat check to his lawyer. It was nothing short of absurd and obscene. Would I have done a better job negotiating than our lawyers? The only thing I know for sure is that I couldn't have done any worse. It was a disaster.

The entire episode was immensely frustrating and a total waste of my time. Our senior management assumed that because we were paying our hired guns a ton of money, this would put us in the best position to minimize the damage. It never occurred to our management that expert litigators aren't necessarily skilled negotiators. When you hire lawyers on a noncontingency basis, they get paid their full freight regardless of how badly they mangle the outcome. One of my brothers often reminds me that if someone ends up in bankruptcy court, the lawyers always manage to get paid while everyone else who's owed money gets screwed.

I was a vital defense team member but didn't participate in the resolution strategy since I wasn't a company staff lawyer. After putting it off for over a decade, this ordeal was a primary impetus behind my decision to take the bar examination. Our hired guns provided further incentive when they told me I'd never pass it given the considerable elapsed time since I'd picked up a law book. They had a point since the pass rate of the California exam at that time was well below 50%. Their personal challenge became a giant motivating force behind my quest to crush the exam.

The statement I'm about to make is a generalization based on various lawyers I've dealt with, but it certainly doesn't apply to all lawyers and doesn't necessarily apply to most lawyers. I obviously have no idea if it applies to your lawyer. Here it is: Despite their depiction in movies and television and the general perception promoted by the legal industry, lawyers are less effective negotiators than people I've worked with in other disciplines, such as program management, purchasing, and contract administration. Don't automatically trust your lawyer to negotiate effectively on your behalf. I'm sure that statement will come as a shock to a lot of people, including most of the legal community of which I'm a member. Would you allow an electrician to install new plumbing for you? If not, think twice about allowing an attorney to negotiate for you.

I was a negotiator long before I thought about taking a bar exam. After I conquered two of them, I continued doing the same type of work I'd been doing all along. I never spent one day practicing as a lawyer and have never considered myself to be one. However, having that knowledge and experience behind me qualifies me to evaluate lawyers and their ability to negotiate for their clients.

If you need a lawyer to represent you in a matter involving high-stakes negotiating, ask lots of questions. Ask about other cases like yours, what each side wanted, and what each side eventually got. Ask to see his track record. Ask for references. Ask for background information demonstrating successful performance in negotiating favorable settlements in cases that could have gone either way. A law degree from Yale or Harvard does not signify or demonstrate negotiating prowess. Not by a long shot.

A great swimmer isn't necessarily a great water polo player. A great rugby player isn't necessarily a great football player. In both instances, the reverse is also true. Specialized skills apply to every sport and are not necessarily transferable at the same level of competence. Only a handful of athletes have competed at the professional level in two sports, and the results in their secondary sport were usually nothing to write home about. None of them lasted very long, either. The upshot is that legal skills and negotiating skills are not interchangeable and never have been.

Do your due diligence before hiring a lawyer. Satisfy yourself that you've chosen someone with the needed skills and who will be your best advocate for negotiating real estate deals, divorce disputes, and civil litigations involving significant amounts of money. How many people entrust cases involving vast sums of money to lawyers who say they can negotiate but are inept when confronted by someone who actually can?

I understand why people assume that lawyers are skilled negotiators. They've been swayed by what they see and hear in the media about lawyers representing clients who scored settlements in the millions. There's an overabundance of advertising touting lawyers who will get you what you deserve in class action lawsuits totaling hundreds of millions. They see lawyers in action in movies and television shows who appear to know how to wheel and deal with the opposition while overlooking that it's all scripted and will always play out the way the writers intended.

Since perception invariably trumps reality, the impression is firmly planted in the viewer's mind that lawyers, by default, make good negotiators. Some are terrible negotiators and could cost you serious money if they're not up to the task you hired them to do.

I Can't Do It!

When I make an offer or counteroffer, I anticipate rejection. I expect to hear "no," "no way," or "I can't accept it." In the unlikely event my offer is accepted, my gut reaction is one of shock and that I offered too much. I was more generous than I should have been. I should have known better than to give away the store, and I'll never do that again—famous last words.

If I only had a nickel for every time I've heard someone tell me they can't move, can't budge, can't bend, or can't go any higher or lower. I hear it, but I'm not listening. While all those statements project an air of finality, don't be fooled.

Pretend you've made a counteroffer as a buyer, and the response is, "I can't accept it. I can't go that low." Ask yourself what they mean by "can't." The last thing you should do is assume they're done negotiating. Whatever you do, don't make another offer, thereby bidding against yourself.

When I'm told "no," what I hear is that negotiations have just begun. Understanding this apparent contradiction requires a bit of reverse psychology and appreciating that some negotiation tactics are counterintuitive. People tend to get more defensive when pressured to say "yes" than when left with the option to say "no." Saying "yes" requires an acknowledgment and commitment that the matter under discussion has reached a point of finality. Any disagreement before that point ceases to be an issue and is no longer a subject for further debate.

Saying "no" is far more powerful and evokes a sense of control and security when told what to do. It's human nature for people to resist being told what to do, regardless of the circumstances. I expect that whatever I propose will be rejected and followed by further discussion and a possible counteroffer. Once the power of "no" has been exercised, the other party will become more relaxed, open to constructive dialogue, and more likely to explicitly define what they want. They've stood their ground, have not backed down, and have scored a victory in their eyes. Now, the business of real negotiating can begin.

When someone says they can't do something, it signals that I may have hit an inflection point in their plan that I need to break through, similar to a resistance level or moving average for a common stock. The first order of business is to figure out precisely what they mean by their language. Here's my list of possible meanings for "I can't" do something.

- I won't do it
- I don't want to do it
- I'm unable to do it
- I'm physically incapable of doing it
- I don't know how to do it
- I don't have the necessary skills to do it
- I'm prevented from doing it
- I'm not authorized to do it

The word "can't" in the context of a negotiation means nothing to me. It's simply a dodge or decoy designed to make me believe something to be true that's seldom true. I've heard it hundreds of times; I ignore it and pretend it never happened.

Anyone with children has experienced this more times than they can remember. If you ask a child to do his chores and he says he can't, it rarely means he's incapable of doing them. Chances are he doesn't want to do them, but he uses the word "can't" as a way of deflecting from the truth. It's an obscure way of lying without overtly blurting it out. Call it a diplomatic white lie with a motive.

When someone confronts you and says they "can't" do something, you must determine what they mean. None of the possibilities on my list mean the same thing, although people are sometimes tricked into thinking they do. The takeaway is that words matter in a negotiation, and they matter a lot. We don't have to be experts in the English language to understand how true this is. In a letter to the editor published in my local newspaper, I addressed a couple of ways that deceptive wordsmithery is used to confuse and conceal financial reality. Alarmingly, we've more than doubled the national debt since this was written in May 2011.

Government Math Has Its Own Rules

Let's say you are giving your child an allowance of $10. He or she asks for a raise to $15. When you say you will agree to $12, they say you are imposing a "cut" of $3.

Using government math, you cut their allowance from the $15 they wanted down to only $12. Using the math that I learned a half-century ago, you raised their allowance from $10 to $12.

Remember how government math works when you hear politicians talk about draconian spending cuts.

Politicians use the same trickery when they talk about the debt. When they say they are "cutting the deficit," you might think they are reducing our cumulative national debt of $14 trillion to some lesser number. Not even close.

What "cutting the deficit" really means is that they will slightly reduce the rate at which that $14 trillion is going up. So, a $100 billion deficit cut this year means that our current $14 trillion debt will increase to $15.4 trillion instead of $15.5 trillion.

Does that sound like a "cut" to you?

Don't allow yourself to be fooled into believing that differences in language can be easily explained away by semantics or misunderstandings. If I tell you during negotiations that I can't go any lower, don't assume I mean what I say. Like it or not, deception and concealment are necessary elements of competent negotiating.

One way to make this determination is to ask what they mean. Couch the question to preclude any confusion or misconceptions about their position. I do my best to circumvent the direct approach because I don't want an answer that might lock them into a position they can't easily back away from.

An example of what I'm getting at is illustrated by analyzing how juries function. It's common practice for juries to take a vote soon after starting deliberations to determine how close they are to a verdict. At a minimum, the first vote should be by secret ballot. This process allows everyone to see where things stand without publicly committing themselves to one side or the other. Otherwise, people tend to lock themselves into a position regarding guilt or innocence and are unwilling to move off that position even when it becomes apparent they can't adequately defend it. An anonymous vote makes it easier and less embarrassing to change their vote during the initial deliberations that may influence their opinions. Once the deliberations have progressed sufficiently, it makes more sense to ascertain where everyone stands so they can focus on achieving a verdict.

People evade admitting mistakes or that they were wrong about something. I'm not saying they won't change their minds, but it's harder to do once you've locked in your decision. It's human nature.

The same phenomenon occurs in negotiations if one side prematurely plants its flag, intentionally or accidentally. I shun direct questioning if I can find another way to get the answers I seek. One of the methods I use is to engage in conversation that skirts around the central question in hopes I'll discover the context for their response. Years ago, I coined a phrase for this tactic: Reading people with the ancillary question. If I want to know how someone thinks, I won't ask them how they think. Instead, I might ask them for their opinion on a current event. I'm not interested in their opinion as much as how they arrived at their opinion. That tells me how they process information to reach a judgment or conclusion. That insight is valuable in a negotiation because it helps me anticipate what they'll do in response to whatever I do.

When negotiations stall because the other side says they're stuck and can't move, assess if this is a temporary impasse or a deadlock. How you do that depends on the state of the negotiations and what your gut tells you. I have few options if they've rejected my last offer, and I've determined they're stuck. One is to walk away, a tactic I discussed in a previous chapter. It could jolt them into reconsidering their position. Another is to restate my prior offer and tell them it's my best and final offer. Whether I choose to do the latter isn't a decision I plan for in advance, and I rarely do it as a bluff.

In a forthcoming chapter about two instances where I sued to resolve disputes, I did so because the other parties would not budge from positions I considered indefensible. They said they couldn't negotiate, and I knew they could. I never would have sued if I doubted their ability to keep negotiating. It was the only way I could put enough pressure on them to back down, and both cases were settled without stepping foot in a courtroom. The other parties didn't know or figure out that I had virtually no leverage in either case. Sometimes, it pays to be bold, but you must also be confident that you'll prevail.

In the overwhelming majority of negotiations I've done, suing was never a consideration. I exerted pressure through various means depending on the circumstances I was facing. Most often, it was based on knowing the other party had to get a deal, and there was schedule urgency to make it happen without extended delay. Sometimes, I walked away and pretended I didn't care if nothing happened, and we all went home with nothing. Use whatever leverage you have, and if you don't have much, create it by whatever means are available.

In negotiations, as in life in general, perceptions are usually far more important than reality. If the other party believes I'm about to walk away from a negotiation, that belief will influence their behavior even if I have no intentions of doing it. Power derives from the other party's belief that you have leverage even when you don't.

Mediation for Dispute Resolution

Mediation requires a divergent mindset from negotiation. I only realized how incisive this divergence is once I completed mediator training under the bar association continuing legal education program. I began the training believing my negotiation skill set could be rolled into mediation, giving me a leg up on completing the course. Those hopes withered away once we started digging into the nuts and bolts of the mediation process. The first order of business was to suppress my default mode of thinking like a negotiator. That turned out to be much more challenging than I had anticipated.

Mediation is a desirable method for resolving legal disputes, but it can also resolve a multitude of conflicts and disagreements. Most disputes are settled before initiating lawsuits, and relatively few end up in court. If that weren't true, we'd need more courtrooms, judges, and other legal professionals to handle the enormous caseload burden. A mediator can be engaged at any point in the process, including at the beginning. No rule says you have to wait until you're deadlocked in a stalemate before blowing the calvary horn.

I've made it clear that I don't go into any negotiation expecting to compromise, but mediation flips that assertion on its head. Mediation, to varying degrees, relies conceptually on compromise to succeed. Both sides have to make concessions, or the mediator won't be able to catalyze progress toward bringing them closer together. One tangible benefit of mediation is that it's far less costly than going to trial. However, a trial provides some measure of finality when a judgment is rendered either at the trial level or, ultimately, on appeal. No such assurance exists with mediation, which can drag on forever without reaching a definitive conclusion.

There are significant advantages to mediation that deserve careful consideration. It puts the power in the hands of the two parties rather than a judge or jury. It's purely voluntary and nonbinding unless and until both parties arrive at an agreement. They have total control over the outcome. Unlike arbitration, you're under no obligation to agree to anything you don't like, even if that would result in ending the dispute.

The appointment of a mediator is subject to the approval of both parties. The mediator is powerless to make decisions related to the dispute but performs essential functions designed to facilitate and moderate the debate. These include setting the framework and ground rules for the discussions, encouraging open and constructive communications, ensuring complete confidentiality, monitoring the unfolding process, and promoting fairness and professionalism throughout the proceedings. Ideally, the mediator will enjoy a reputation for credibility and trust necessary to gain the confidence of both parties. They must be convinced that he will consistently exhibit flexibility and impartiality and never show favoritism toward either side.

The mediator takes on the role of a neutral third party responsible for building common ground and providing independent evaluations of the respective positions of both parties. Unlike negotiators, they're not advocates and must foster a climate of objectivity, self-determination, and direct participation. They perform a highly sensitive function, and if they don't execute their obligations to the expectations of both sides, the entire process will likely collapse in failure.

The mediator establishes the agenda and constructs a roadmap to help guide the participants to a potential solution. Once underway, the process consists of both parties presenting their accounts of what has transpired. This usually leads to individualized, confidential caucusing followed by shuttling between the parties to offer suggestions and creative alternatives to reframe the discussion.

The mediator is in a position to alter the perceptions of what led to the dispute by reformulating the events in a neutral setting without any pressure to agree or disagree. Coercion is not to be substituted for persuasion. The objective is to preserve the respective parties' needs and interests, not the mediator's self-interests. Maintaining absolute neutrality is more demanding than it sounds and can make the mediator's job stressful and burdensome.

Mediation can grind to a halt when the parties become so committed to their respective positions that it becomes impossible to budge them. This recalcitrance also manifests in negotiations, especially when both sides believe they've already conceded more than their share and decide to dig in and retreat to their bunkers. A stalemate is very likely without a mediator or third party to intervene at that point.

A mediator can shift the process to seeking solutions based on the merits and respective interests rather than positional posturing that's going nowhere. It's not unusual for needs and interests to collide with concrete wants and desires. A classic example of this is the parable of the orange cited earlier. As a refresher, two people claim ownership of the same orange, so they settle their dispute by cutting it in half. They later discover that one wanted the juice and the other wanted the rind, but it was too late, so neither party got what they wanted.

A disinterested third party could have separated the parties from the problem at hand and forged a path that would have satisfied both sides. One way to accomplish this is to compile a consolidated list of their genuine needs and interests. In the process, ask simple questions. Why do you want the orange? What do you intend to do with the orange? What happens if you don't get the orange? Then, refocus the discussion toward potential options and impartial recommendations to reconcile their interests and achieve a resolution. By steering the conversation, the third party can effectively limit the number and uncertainty of future decisions and assist both parties in understanding their decisions' impact on the final result.

In this example, the mediator would have discovered that one party wanted the juice and the other wanted the rind. Rather than halving the orange, that solution is recommended to both sides and is contingent on their approval. They can provide consent, feedback, and constructive criticism of the proposed plan. This process exposes which interests and priorities are in concert and conflict. That approach tends to diffuse and soften obstacles that surface due to personal and emotional resistance. Here, neither side has to concede anything. It becomes a joint decision they both want. Problem solved.

Far more complex international and multilateral negotiations have employed this technique. When there are many diverse participants, they tend to defend their turf without understanding the ramifications to all the parties. It's complicated to assimilate all the individual pieces and attempt to get an agreement that satisfies everyone. An alternative is for a third party to create a draft agreement that incorporates the common elements of all those pieces and highlights their shared interests. This draft becomes the working document that all parties can critique and criticize while identifying objections and areas of consent. Eventually, the goal is to arrive at a coordinated position representing their unified agreement.

The mediation process enables the rapid identification and isolation of what's causing a dispute. It provides tremendous insight into the strengths and theories of both parties and may influence how they view their chances of prevailing in a legal battle. Whereas a trial ordinarily results in a win for one side and a loss for the other, mediation allows the exploration of nuanced solutions that may benefit both sides. Also, mediation doesn't restrict you to the limited court-imposed remedies usually available according to the applicable law.

Mediation contrasts sharply with the contentious atmosphere of a courtroom where the risk of getting an unfavorable verdict is always present. The legal system doesn't guarantee justice will be served, and you can spend massive amounts of money for a ruling you didn't want. If your negotiation efforts have failed to produce acceptable results, mediation is something to consider as a component of your overall risk analysis. A valuable potential upside is the preservation of the personal relationships of the vying parties.

Sometimes, You May Have to Sue

Legal action is a last resort because it demonstrates a failure on my part to persuade the person or company I'm suing to appreciate the merits of my position. Suing was never an option during my business career, so I never considered it. I devoted too much time, money, and energy to my professional negotiations to squander it all in a courtroom where the attorneys always seem to make a killing. When complex negotiations involving hundreds of millions of dollars are on the line, you find a way to get a deal. Somehow, in some way, you get it done.

It hasn't always played out that way in my personal life, and I attribute this to several factors. The primary one is that when a private individual negotiates with a large company, that company knows it has significant leverage over you by default. The company may have attorneys on staff trained to make problems go away before they escalate, and they want to avoid setting precedents that may come back to bite them in the future.

Over the years, I've filed two lawsuits in small claims court. In both instances, I did everything possible to settle before filing. Nothing worked. Neither of these suits involved significant amounts of money, but I decided to sue on principle. I don't like being squeezed by companies that believe they can get away with it, and I don't like being taken advantage of because I'm the little guy who should shut up and take it. When faced with such a situation, the companies don't know who they're dealing with, but I'm determined to make sure they find out.

The first suit involved a 2002 automobile I bought used in a 2006 private sale. The car had a basic warranty covering parts and workmanship defects for three years or 36,000 miles, whichever came first. That warranty had already expired, but there's a separate five-year limited warranty for rust perforation covering the repair or replacement of any original body panel that rusts through from the inside out. This warranty has no mileage limitation and would cover my damage if it qualified as perforated rust.

The warranty provisions include a long list of exclusions that would not be covered. My damage was on the engine hood in an area where rust would not usually appear that soon. I didn't know if the previous owner had done something to the vehicle that might have triggered or accelerated rust formation on the hood. Lacking any expertise in metals or rust, I wasn't sure if my damage would qualify under the extended paint warranty. When faced with uncertainty such as this, my approach is always the same. If the worst that can happen is they say no, I have nothing to lose by pursuing a claim, then watching what happens.

I took my car to the nearest dealer to inspect the damage. The service manager took photos that the dealership manager later reviewed. Several days later, I received a phone call informing me the extended paint warranty for rust perforation did not apply, and the basic warranty had already expired. The bottom line was that I would have to pay for the repair.

I told the dealer I wanted to appeal its decision without knowing if such an appeal was possible. My action illustrates a critical point. In such situations, too many people ask for something rather than saying they want something. I don't ask for anything because it implies I need someone's consent. If you ask me for something in the middle of a dispute, I'll probably deny it. Instead, tell me why you want it and are entitled to it. Put yourself on offense and stop playing defense. It's more than just a psychological distinction. You're far more likely to shape the outcome you want when you take the initiative to make it happen. Don't wait for anyone else to suddenly decide that your position has merit and advocate on your behalf. It's no time to be subtle or submissive.

The dealer agreed to convey my appeal to the manufacturer but expected its decision would be confirmed. I'd present the appeal directly to the regional warranty manager responsible for many dealerships in the surrounding area. The dealer wasn't bluffing, and I knew my chances of winning an appeal were nearly nonexistent. Regardless, I had two reasons for appealing the decision. First, I wanted to ensure he knew I was serious about my claim. Second, if my claim ended up in court, I'd be able to tell the judge I exhausted all avenues of resolution and that suing was my last resort. The judge won't be sympathetic to your case if he determines you could have solved it by simply trying harder.

It's incumbent on you to pursue every reasonable route to finding a solution, no matter how steadfast the person you're dealing with happens to be. Remedies available in small claims courts depend on the jurisdiction but are typically limited to monetary damages or the return of property. Other forms of equitable relief may only be available if you bring suit in the next-level state court.

I brought my car in again on the date when the regional warranty manager was available. He inspected the damage, took more photos, and said he would render a decision within a couple of days. As expected, he called to reaffirm that no warranty coverage was available.

I was prepared for rejection but made my case for why it should be covered even though I had virtually no leverage. My position was that the source of the rust was an open question, so I offered to share the repair cost with the manufacturer. The warranty manager was dug in and wouldn't give an inch. I continued to press him hard, but it was clear that his hands were tied. I had to go over his head to higher management or regroup and pursue an alternate plan. When our call concluded, I sensed he was confident the case was closed. Not a chance. I was already considering other options to incentivize him to reverse his decision.

One action I could have taken during our call would be threatening a lawsuit. Sometimes this works to loosen things up, and sometimes it doesn't. However, I would never level a threat against someone who doesn't have the power and authority to react to it on behalf of the company. I'll illustrate what I mean with a simple example. I buy something at a large department store, and a few days later, I return it. I find the store clerk I bought it from and ask for a refund. He tells me my item is not eligible for a refund under their return policy. I won't respond by saying I'm prepared to sue the store for my money because I'd be wasting my time and his. Such a threat should be directed at the store manager with the requisite authority to act, one way or another. Ideally, I'd do it in person because it would generate a more immediate and pronounced effect than other methods.

I follow a few self-imposed rules regarding business communication methods. I believe in what I refer to as "method reciprocity" based on the means used by the initiator of the communication. If someone sends me an email, I reply with an email. If someone leaves me a telephone message, I call them back. If someone sends me a handwritten letter, I respond with a handwritten letter. And so it goes. I employ this approach in all my negotiations unless I have an exceptional reason not to.

There are a few reasons why I do this. The most obvious is that it's easy and requires no thinking on my part, and it's common courtesy to maintain the same level of formality established by the initiator. If I receive a signed, certified letter from someone, what kind of hidden message am I sending if I respond with an email or text message? I can envision employing this strategy if I'm displeased with the letter. I'd fire off a quick email to categorically dismiss the letter's contents. However, that would be an exception to my general rule of respecting the initiator's communication method.

Being the initiator allows me to choose the method most beneficial to my goals. My overwhelming preference is to communicate and negotiate in person whenever possible. While I'll always document the results in writing, most of the communication up to that point will be verbal in face-to-face sessions. As things progress, there will likely be phone calls between meetings, and I'll also make a summary record of those.

While I rarely use a communication method that is less formal than the initiator, I'll raise the level of formality under certain conditions. For example, if I have a dispute with a company about a warranty issue and it sends me a boilerplate email denying my claim, I won't respond with an email. Instead, I'll send a certified letter with a return receipt and elevate the recipient to someone in senior management. If I can't figure out which executive to transmit it to, I'll send it to the president or CEO. While neither will personally read my letter, someone on their staff will read it, and they won't be able to pretend they never received it. If I have little leverage, this may be the best way of getting someone's attention. The recipient will treat a certified letter more seriously than a regular letter, email, or text message.

Of course, the other party has no obligation to follow my self-imposed communication methodology. If they don't, I still maintain the same process. In responding to them, I'll mirror whatever they do unless I have a compelling reason not to.

Getting back to my warranty dispute, threatening or suing the dealer was never on the table. Automobile warranties are issued and controlled by the manufacturer's corporate headquarters, and I filed a claim against it in small claims court. An added benefit to this approach is that the manufacturer has the deepest pockets to pay monetary damages. To determine the claim amount, I went to a reputable collision repair shop and asked for a firm quote to repair and repaint my engine hood. The hood is removable, so the rest of the car doesn't require shielding. The repair and painting are simple, straightforward tasks, and the quote plus court costs totaled slightly over $500.

Since I had no conclusive evidence that the damage was the type of rust covered by the extended warranty, I thought my chances of winning were a toss-up. There was also no conclusive evidence to the contrary. It was my opinion against theirs, and I assumed they had a stable of experts who could defend their position. I thought about hiring an expert but elected not to. An expert might not help my case, and the cost would exceed my claim. My leverage was minimal, and I racked my brain to generate ideas to improve it.

I ultimately calculated that the manufacturer would not respond to the suit because of the legal fees it would incur and the considerable cost of going to trial in a state across the country. Then, there was the plausible risk it would lose. The bill for all that would be significantly more than the cost of repairing my hood. Given the small size of my claim, I was counting on their risk assessment to prompt a reconsideration of the initial rejection. A good business decision often takes precedence over getting entangled in a process that might result in a legal decision that works against you.

While my quote from an independent collision shop was around $500, the dealer's repair cost was far less because it had an on-site paint shop. The people employed in that shop were getting paid whether they had work to do or not. So, the net cost of a small job like mine was primarily for the paint and labor for the rust repair. I estimated their actual cost to be at most $250. Big car companies usually don't go to court over that amount, and I was counting on it in my case.

I filed the suit and waited to see what would happen. A couple of weeks later, I received a call from the dealer's service manager to inform me they wanted to take another look at my car. Bingo. Within a week, I had a freshly painted engine hood that perfectly matched the existing paint. Once that happened, my final act was to officially withdraw the lawsuit.

Would you have given up after the warranty manager told you they wouldn't pay? If so, you might be part of the majority who would. I might have conceded if not for my high confidence that they'd cave first. It's one more game of chicken, and I admit I like to win more than I like to lose. Before deciding whether or not you'll sue, analyze the costs and risks to both parties. Compare them under competing postures of each side winning while the other loses, then draw realistic conclusions. Suing is an option when it's your last resort, and you have at least an even chance of prevailing.

I'll never know what would have happened had my case gone to trial. The manufacturer could have brought in experts to testify that this was not rust perforation. The warranty expressly excludes any damage that started on the exterior surface. I'd produce an expert to testify they were wrong, setting up a battle of the experts. My biggest fear was I'd get a judge who was a car expert, and he'd demand to inspect my car personally. That could either be good or bad for me, but it was a risk I didn't ignore. In the final analysis, I accepted that no one could be certain one way or the other, so I'd take my chances by testing the resolve of the manufacturer and its willingness to go to battle.

I offer one last thought on this episode. If you decide to sue over a dispute similar to mine, don't be greedy. If the damages clearly exceed what's reasonable under the circumstances, your chances of a courtroom face-off are much higher. In my case, I could have sued for the cost of repainting the entire car to ensure a perfect color-match. By limiting my claim to the engine hood, I handed them a number that slid under the radar and gave me what I wanted without an extended dogfight. I believe it was obvious to them that I hadn't concocted a scheme to get more out of my claim than I was entitled to. I was happy and they were happy. Case closed.

The second lawsuit was more complicated, and the underlying facts worked against me. I'd become concerned about traveling with my Rolex, especially outside the U.S. Getting through security checkpoints and customs routinely required removing the watch so I could pass through the metal detectors. Sending it through scanners took it out of my eyesight, and I worried that what went in one end would not come out the other. Random personal scans via a wand or other means only added to the time when it was out of my sight. There was no way I would pack it in my check-in or carry-on luggage. Add that to the likelihood that I was a target for theft in many parts of the world, and I decided it had become too risky to wear on future air travel.

I bought a much less expensive Luminox watch from a retailer in New York City with a physical and online presence. It maintains a website with an extensive selection of authentic watches at heavily discounted prices, but there's a catch. The company buys excess inventory from manufacturers at below-wholesale prices and sells them to consumers without a manufacturer warranty. To compensate for the lack of warranty coverage, the retailer provides one that is less comprehensive than the manufacturer's and limits its overall liability. If something goes wrong with your watch, the retailer will repair or replace it for a defined period based on the particular brand. Their policy provides no refunds or exchanges due to their competitively low pricing.

Buried in the fine print is what would happen if your watch couldn't be repaired or replaced. In that event, the retailer issues a "store credit" to purchase another watch. I bought the model I wanted with a complete understanding of the store policy. About a year later, the watch stopped and restarted several times for no apparent reason. I returned it and subsequently discovered it was defective and not repairable. In addition, the model I purchased had been discontinued and was irreplaceable, so I would be issued a credit for the amount paid.

I searched the store's website for a similar watch made by the same company. I discovered that 95% of their watches were out of stock, and the few available models were unacceptable to me. All of them looked starkly different from the one I bought. I contacted the retailer, asked for a refund, and was told my only option was a store credit.

At this point, I had to make a decision. Will I take the store credit even though all the watches I was interested in were unavailable, or do I take one last shot at resolving the dispute peacefully? The seller was acting unreasonably, given the severe lack of inventory. Nevertheless, the seller ignored all my demands. Most retailers I've dealt with would exercise discretion and waive restrictive policies when it made good business sense. I decided to take one last shot at presenting formal arguments in a businesslike manner.

The following text from the documents I sent to the seller illustrates the preparation needed if you're contemplating a warranty battle. Keep detailed records of all facts, dates, documents, and the chronology of events. Reality is far different from what you see on television depicting how small claims courts operate. If you're serious and expect to win, you must prepare. It better positions you to settle favorably before trial and solidifies a much stronger case if you land in court.

On 06 September 2016, I demanded a full refund payment by 20 September. When nothing happened, I sent the following message to the seller on 21 September.

> I did not receive the refund for my defective Luminox watch by 20 September as requested in my message dated 06 September. The attached PDF document explains what's coming. I'm certain your legal counsel would be interested in seeing it soon. I don't settle winning lawsuits once I've gone through the time, trouble, and expense of filing them.

Text of the PDF document referred to in my message:

Description of Claim (Order #941483—G. Michael) 21 September 2016

Breach of warranties on a Luminox man's wristwatch purchased from [seller].

Timeline/Date

- 01 Nov 14: Order #941483 placed for Luminox Space Blue Dial Watch (5023). Total cost is $291.18.

- 02 Dec 15: The watch stops for about 30 minutes and restarts for no apparent reason. This pattern is repeated several times over the following two months.

- 28 Jan 16: The watch is returned to the seller for warranty repair or replacement.

- 05 Feb 16: Seller confirms receipt of the watch via email and assigns Service #272211. The email states: "Please keep in mind that the repair time can be up to eight weeks."

- Feb–Aug 16: No feedback from the seller about the watch for 30 weeks.

- 29 Aug 16 : I contacted the seller to learn the watch's status. The seller representative promises to find out and call back.

- 29 Aug 16: I received a telephone message from the seller, which is partially quoted here: "Unfortunately, it seems like the watch was not able to be repaired. We did have it sent out to a Luminox service center because we were not able to do it here, and they deemed the watch to just be defective and not repairable, so what we're offering instead is a store credit of the amount you paid $291.18."

- 30-31 Aug 16: Since the watch I returned can't be repaired or replaced, I searched the seller's website for other possible Luminox watches. I inquired if model XA.9401 is available.

- 06 Sep 16: The seller's sales manager informed me that model XA.9401 is unavailable. I rechecked the seller's website, which displayed only two Luminox watches, neither of which is acceptable to me. I request a full refund via email to purchase the watch I want elsewhere. The seller's sales manager tells me via email that this order is only eligible for a store credit. Since none of the watches offered were acceptable to me, I sent a demand via email: "Send me a full refund by check no later than 20 September 2016, or I'll file suit." The sales manager responds via email: "This is not eligible for a refund."

- 21 Sep 16: I emailed this claim summary to the seller's sales manager and suggested that he forward it to the seller's legal counsel.

Claim Summary Narrative

As stated by the seller representative in a phone message received on 29 August 16, the watch was defective when sold. The manufacturer's authorized Luminox service center determined this; its conclusion is not disputed. Further, it was impossible for me to discover the defect.

This sale breached the express warranty and the implied warranty of merchantability. The seller claims that my only remedy is a store credit of $291.18 to purchase a different watch. This resolution would be satisfactory if other Luminox models on the seller's website were acceptable replacements. They are not because similar replacements are out of stock.

The seller has forced me to purchase something I don't want by imposing a store credit rather than a refund. I'm being penalized for unknowingly purchasing a defective watch that can't be repaired or replaced. When a product is defective and does not perform its intended function, I do not have to accept a store credit.

Remedy

The seller has refused to refund my purchase price, so my only recourse is to sue in [state] small claims court. The amount of my claim will exceed the purchase price. The claim will also include all costs associated with the lawsuit, including court-assessed fees and legal expenses related to my pursuit and resolution of this claim.

Based on the seller's refusal to refund my money, it would prefer to risk paying more due to losing a lawsuit.

Service of process to:

[Seller's agent]

New York, New York

Filing suit can be done electronically with the form included on the following two pages. I've retained all the email correspondence and recorded telephone message for trial.

If this dispute went to court and I were held to the provisions of the store's repair or replace policy, I would lose. I told the store manager that ordinarily, I wouldn't question its policy, but when 95% of the watches are out of stock, strict enforcement of its policy was unfair and dubious at best. He should show some flexibility based on these unique circumstances, particularly when he couldn't assure me the watches I was interested in would be restocked in the future.

I was willing to negotiate, but the store was not. I told the manager I would sue, hoping this would prompt him to reconsider. He didn't, and he had the authority to decide what the store would do next. Only make such a threat to someone with the requisite power of position. Based purely on my intuition and experience, he thought I was bluffing. I wasn't. Untold numbers of people threaten to sue and never follow through and do it. I've been known to bluff when it was the optimal tactical move, but this wasn't one of those times. In this instance, their policy was patently unfair.

With only two exceptions, every time I've had a dispute like this, I've been able to negotiate what I wanted without filing a claim in court. In this case, I was doing it purely on principle since the money involved was relatively small. It bothered me that the store also asserted that it would enforce its policy even if an entire brand was sold out, forcing me to choose a different brand. That's not how I'd do business with a new customer with a potential for more sales in the future.

While I believed my case could go either way in court, I was banking on the store's attorneys to shut it down based on the small claim amount, associated litigation costs, and the risk it might lose. They never responded to the complaint, and the court issued a default judgment that included the actual cost of the watch, all court fees, and compensation for the time I spent pursuing the claim. I'd receive about three times the cost of the watch, so the store's decision to call my "bluff" was not a good one. I reminded them of that after I received my check. I couldn't resist rubbing it in. They deserved it. Then, with all that "free" money in hand, I bought a much better watch.

I include this story to crystallize a critical point. While negotiating has always been my preferred method of settling disputes like this, sometimes you'll run into a brick wall with no way around or through it. Even if you don't have an ironclad case that would be a slam dunk in court, suing the other party puts them in a position of doing a risk assessment that may not be as obvious as it seems to you. If you believe you've been wronged in a substantial way that offers no other recourse, filing a small claim induces significant leverage to force a settlement without going to court. Most companies don't want to go to battle unless your claim is frivolous and without merit. Otherwise, their best option is to cut a deal that will make you happy and preserve their reputation for fair dealing.

Before exercising the legal system, I did everything I could to negotiate a settlement. I encourage everyone to do the same. If I had thought my likelihood of prevailing had ever been less than 50%, I would have taken a different course. Reasonable people can solve disagreements without escalating into a major dispute, but when you can't make that happen for whatever reason, you have every right to defend your position.

A legitimate question is whether this is a justifiable use of our legal system. The courts are overwhelmed with cases, burdening all the staff and taxpayers who pay their salaries. We have a right to expect that cases coming into the system are worthy of the time and effort of everyone involved. My two cases were only important to me and were each less than $1,000. At the bottom line, neither case burdened the legal system since both were resolved before trial. In addition, both defendants paid the court fees as part of the settlement, so there was zero cost to the taxpayers.

We can also debate the ethics and advisability of threatening to sue, but neither instance was an idle threat. Using this tactic is nothing new and happens frequently. Although it's impossible to prove, the threat is exercised far more often than filing a lawsuit. The benefit is that the threat, if perceived as authentic, is often enough to compel an expeditious settlement. This undoubtedly saves court time and reduces the legal fees for all the parties involved.

Sometimes, merely the hint of suing is enough to force a satisfactory conclusion. The cost of my new refrigerator was open to downward adjustment under specific conditions. I was entitled to a refund of the difference between what I paid and any advertised sale price, up until seven days after delivery to my home. Within a few days of the delivery, I discovered a sale was underway and fired off a letter to the manufacturer's customer service department. Based on the price differential, I requested a refund of $400 and backed it up with supporting documentation.

Although my letter was dated and mailed six days following delivery, the manufacturer denied the refund. Without spelling out the details of its rationale, I didn't hesitate to challenge the decision. When my challenge crashed and burned, and my subsequent appeal to higher management went up in flames, I sent a final message: "Please provide me with the name and address of the authorized agent who receives service of process on behalf of your company for all legal matters. I'll need that information if I opt to pursue this matter in small claims court."

Bingo. That was all it took to shake loose my refund. While a tactic like this won't always work, you've got nothing to lose by trying it.

Personal Negotiations

In the "Introduction" section of this book, I made this assertion: We all conduct dozens of negotiations every day in our personal and professional lives, sometimes without being conscious that they're taking place. Most people negotiate within their family, not in a business setting. This is especially true if they have children. A major facet of raising a child who's old enough to understand the concept of give-and-take is recognizing that discipline is not always something a parent can unilaterally dictate. A hardline approach to instilling discipline in a child works until it doesn't, more so as they age. Circumstances sometimes require flexibility and a willingness to accommodate their feelings and desires if you can do it in a way that doesn't marginalize your parental role.

Every family has a unique dynamic, so offering generalized advice has obvious, significant drawbacks. What works for one may or may not work for another. My perspective is based on personal observation, and that's all it represents. There's no science behind any of it, but here are some pointers I encourage you to consider. They are in no way limited to use within the family unit. I follow these principles in my daily interactions, regardless of who I engage with.

Choose your confrontations carefully, and remember that your words and actions have long-term consequences. Compromise becomes far more difficult to achieve once you've crossed the line from rational thought to chronic agitation.

Be honest even when the other party completely disagrees with your position. To negotiate successfully, accurately state what you want, leaving no room for confusion or unfounded assumptions. This may be painful at the outset, but the truth will come out eventually and result in even more pain. This approach applies to both sides. Only when you know precisely where you stand can you attain progress in resolving differences.

Don't be fooled into thinking that threats are a way to exercise leverage you might think you possess. While leverage is an unfailingly powerful ally, your ability to maximize that advantage depends heavily on how you use it. If you're threatening someone to see things your way, I can almost guarantee they won't see things your way. A better tactic is to make promises you intend to keep, even if you know they aren't immediately acceptable to the other party. This becomes a starting point from which you can move forward to close the gaps between your respective positions. You have to start somewhere, and threatening each other will only worsen the divide and prolong the agony.

Listening too much is never a problem. Talking too much is almost always a problem. Let's face it. When things get heated, the temptation is to talk down and over the other side if necessary. It doesn't work. One of the most effective negotiation tools is to remain silent at strategic junctures, especially when the other party fully expects you to say something. They don't know what to make of that or how to react and wonder if it's due to something they said. They second-guess what preceded your silence and try to dissect the conversation leading up to that point. It's a positive for your side when you're causing the other party to start questioning themselves for no apparent reason. Listen carefully to the reasoning and rationale for their position and ensure that you fully understand their priorities. To prove it, spell them out and repeat them. Ask that they do the same for you.

Concessions that don't irreversibly harm either side may facilitate conflict resolution. The ability to read people helps determine the basic needs the other party will be unable or unwilling to give up. It's typically something less than they'll admit until there's no other way to reach an agreement. It's incumbent on you to figure out what they need at the bottom line before you get to that stage of the negotiation. Use this knowledge to guide the outcome to an acceptable solution that benefits you most. Once you concede something, it's difficult to get it back, if not impossible.

While resolving disputes is adversarial, you don't have to be combative or antagonistic to defend your position and attain the best result. When trying to persuade someone to your way of thinking, they'll be more receptive if the atmosphere is cordial and exhibits mutual respect. While the bombastic approach makes headlines and finds its way into movies and television shows, I've never found it effective. When I'm facing off against a hostile party, I view it as advantageous to my position since they're more likely to make mistakes and concessions that wouldn't otherwise happen.

Don't lock yourself into a position that inhibits a more creative solution from evolving. What seems like an off-the-wall idea at the beginning often matures and molds itself into a viable way forward that no one initially anticipated. It pays to be open-minded, although the tendency is to commit yourself early in the process, leaving little room for better, more inventive ideas.

Something that comes up frequently in my seminars is the tremendous reluctance to negotiate with doctors, dentists, optometrists, lawyers, accountants, and others who provide professional services. For the fortunate who have insurance coverage, they're not inclined to even think about it. They assume the price is the price, and many of them never see the bills before they're paid unless they have a deductible or copayment. If you need surgery, you schedule the surgery and probably never ask in advance how much it will cost. It's an enviable profession to be in when the cost of your services is not consistently an object of discussion or concern.

You've entrusted your life with your doctor, so I understand the awkwardness and uneasiness that accompany efforts to reduce his bill. Get over it. I'm willing to bet that most doctors don't know what you're charged for various procedures. Have they memorized the current procedural terminology (CPT) codes that precisely identify their activities and associated prices? In addition, contracted rates with government and private insurers vary by region. The amount of billing rate information is considerable, subject to change, and more than anyone can keep track of in their head.

If your doctor is like most, someone in the billing department calculates your bill based on the appropriate CPT codes. Unless the bill is challenged, you and your insurance company will pay whatever rates they assign to your procedures. Chances are that no one will negotiate with you or offer a discount unless you take the initiative. You have to make the first move. What follows are ideas and recommendations on how to go about reducing your medical expenditures. You can also adapt these as needed to reduce the expenses incurred with other professional providers.

The ideal time to discuss discounts is right up front. If you don't have insurance and are prepared to pay cash, this gives you significant leverage. If you have an insurance deductible that you'll be paying out of your pocket, use this leverage as well. I've gotten discounts in the range of 30% to 40% whenever I pay cash. Not once was this ever offered to me. I had to get it. It's your money, so empower yourself. Never pay more than the rates negotiated by insurance companies. You always have the option to challenge a medical bill after receiving it, but you have far less leverage to change it. Unless there's a coding error, other mistake, or it's excessive compared to other providers, it may be too late to negotiate. You won't know for sure until you try.

Do independent research on the going rates in your area by CPT code. This is the ammunition you'll need to bargain for lower rates successfully. Websites, such as Healthcare Blue Book, compile and aggregate cost data you can analyze for comparison purposes. If you schedule a procedure covered by insurance, ascertain the out-of-pocket costs in advance. If you don't have insurance, find out the total cost, including hospitalization and all the associated costs of your specific procedure. Use the information you compile as a bargaining chip in reducing your overall expenses. Unless you make some noise, you'll probably pay the sticker price. The squeaky wheel does get the oil.

In addition to paying cash, you might also score a discount by paying in advance. This eliminates many administrative hassles for doctors, and you'll save anywhere from 10% to 30%. Some dentists offer a one-year or multi-year upfront plan that covers routine examinations, cleanings, and x-rays that will save you money. Another way to reduce your immediate out-of-pocket expense is to negotiate a no-interest, extended payment plan. Avoid billing your credit card whenever possible unless you can pay it off within the first month.

Be open and honest with your doctor about costs. Again, nothing will change if you don't bring the topic up. If you're uncomfortable talking directly with your doctor, arrange to meet with the office or billing manager. They will have insight into how prices are assigned and what discounts you may be eligible to receive. Explain your financial situation, insurance coverage if applicable, and exactly what your deductible costs will be. Take the initiative to thoroughly explore options to reduce your anticipated costs.

I highly recommend negotiating directly with your doctor or staff because you are your best advocate. An alternative is to use the services offered by some state healthcare agencies and non-profit organizations that will act on your behalf. Before you talk to them, formulate a battle plan that lays out your goals, desires, and expectations.

There are many other opportunities to negotiate that too often are overlooked. It's symptomatic of a culture so conditioned to paying the sticker price that cutting it is not even on their radar. One tactic I use with small businesses has been very effective. Understandably, some are reluctant to negotiate because they're concerned the word will spread and other customers will expect the same deal I got.

To avoid that dilemma, I make a preemptive promise that I will keep all negotiation details private. They can choose whether to believe me or not. So far, they always have, and I've never violated that promise. That guarantees I'll get the same consideration as a returning customer.

Secrecy can open doors that might otherwise remain closed, but it requires you to take the initiative and explain your position. If you make a fair and reasonable offer, rejection is the worst that can happen. The likely outcome is acceptance or a more attractive counteroffer than their sticker price. It pays to be creative and willing to engage with the people you do business with. I've been surprised by how many times I've saved money simply because I tried.

Great Leaders Negotiate

When we think of great leaders throughout history, the first people that come to mind are usually political and military. That's a tiny subset of our population, but since the news media focus infinitely more on politicians than the general population, it's no surprise that many people equate politicians with leadership.

Several prominent Americans have worn two hats, serving in the military and later assuming the office of the presidency. Presidents who served as general officers include Washington, Jackson, W. Harrison, Taylor, Pierce, A. Johnson, Grant, Hayes, Garfield, Arthur, B. Harrison, and Eisenhower.

While there are notable exceptions, business leaders don't get the level of media attention showered on politicians. Many prefer to stay out of the limelight and focus on running their businesses and generating value for their employees, customers, and shareholders. One commonality is that negotiation plays a substantial role in their daily activities. People's lives, livelihoods, and significant amounts of money are routinely on the line. Successful leaders must be able to negotiate effectively under a slew of circumstances that may be beyond their control.

Leadership is vital in the military for obvious reasons, but what does negotiation have to do with leading a military unit? After all, ranking officers can issue orders with expectations they'll be carried out unconditionally. Where's the give-and-take in that? Let's draw a bright line between military operations on and off the battlefield and look at two excellent examples from World War II. General George Patton, regarded as one of our greatest field generals, wasn't known for his negotiating skills. But his boss, General Dwight Eisenhower, certainly was.

While Patton's singular mission was to overrun and destroy the enemy, Eisenhower had to hold together an alliance of powerful civilian and military leaders with strong opinions and huge egos on both sides of the Atlantic. This was no easy task, but his ability to keep everyone pointed in the same direction is a testament to his negotiating skills. Think of negotiating as persuading and influencing people to your way of thinking, regardless of rank or position in the organization. Eisenhower understood that whenever possible, issuing orders should be reserved for the battlefield and when otherwise necessary to accomplish the mission.

Eisenhower faced monumental challenges as he prepared for the 1944 Allied landing in France. As part of the strategy for Operation Overlord, his staff developed a bombing plan that would result in many civilian casualties in French coastal towns adjacent to the landing zones. As painful as that outcome would be to Ike and his senior officers, they felt it was necessary to help neutralize the German defenses that would attack the vulnerable Higgins boats approaching the beaches.

British Prime Minister Winston Churchill opposed the bombing plan because of concern for the expected casualties. Great Britain had lost an estimated 50,000 civilians during the early stages of the war. The Battle of Britain was a deadly conflict for daylight air superiority between the Royal Air Force and the Luftwaffe. When the Luftwaffe failed to gain the supremacy it wanted, it began a daily campaign of indiscriminate bombing missions over London during both daylight and nighttime hours. The Blitz caused great devastation to the British people and the city, and Churchill was hesitant to agree to a plan that would put thousands of French citizens directly in the line of fire.

Eisenhower reasoned that the most effective way to get Churchill's backing was to present his plan to the French and explain why it was necessary. He appealed to the leader of Free France, the government-in-exile in London, that supported the resistance to the Nazi occupation of France. He convinced General Charles de Gaulle that implementing the bombing plan would facilitate the airborne and naval assaults at Normandy. It was apparent to de Gaulle that sacrifices endured by his fellow countrymen would be crucial to shredding the yoke of the German stranglehold on his country. Consequently, Churchill deferred to de Gaulle, and Ike's plan ultimately prevailed. This was a classic example of Eisenhower relying on his persuasive powers rather than issuing orders as Supreme Commander of the Allied Expeditionary Force.

On 05 June 1944, the day before the invasion, Eisenhower visited with some of the troops who would participate in the air and sea landings. In one iconic photograph, the general is speaking to a group, including 1st Lt. Wallace Strobel of Company E, 502nd Parachute Infantry Regiment of the 101st Airborne Division Screaming Eagles. Strobel was the jumpmaster on flight 23. One of the reasons for Ike's visit was that Air Chief Marshal Sir Trafford Leigh-Mallory of the Royal Air Force had predicted 80% casualties for the 101st. While the general was there to pump up the troops' morale, he would later say they had a much greater influence on him than he did on them. Their courage and bravery in the face of what they knew would be a decisive and brutal battle was an emotional and inspiring experience he never forgot. He left their encampment believing his decision to launch the invasion that night was the best he could make. His soldiers were the ones doing the persuading.

Authority does have its limits, even in the military. You'll often lead people who are more talented, smarter, stronger, better educated, or more charismatic than you are. Giving them orders will work to a point, but you'll be far more successful if you inspire and motivate them while appealing to their self-interests. We don't call that negotiating, but it's a function of the same skill set and strategic thinking. You may also be called upon to lead people you have no formal authority over. You'll be up to that challenge if you've developed the skills practiced by successful negotiators.

Effective leadership requires the assessment of strengths and weaknesses, team building, open communication, patience, determination, analytical skills, creativity, making sensible concessions, some level of risk-taking, and understanding the long-term view. All of these attributes are routinely utilized in the course of a successful negotiation and apply to leaders in any capacity.

Eisenhower recounted a story from his youth in Kansas that foretold his future reliance on negotiation leverage. When he was five, his family visited his mother's relatives at their farm in Topeka. Ike was curious about the animals and decided to check out the barn, but a large goose blocked his path. Realizing he could not dislodge the goose, he cried until his uncle brought him a broom that he used to force the goose out of his way. Once the goose had run off and the coast was clear, Ike headed for the barn. The lesson learned was that he should always negotiate from a position of strength, a lesson he always remembered.

Eisenhower demonstrated his ability to apply the skill set developed during the war when he became America's 34th president. He warned of the unwarranted influence of the military-industrial complex and effectively separated himself from his prior roles as Supreme Allied Commander in Europe and Army Chief of Staff. He understood that he couldn't order politicians to do things the way he could with his military subordinates, and his wartime experience dealing with Roosevelt, Churchill, Stalin, and many other political leaders served him well as president.

I witnessed the negotiating and leadership skills of a military officer who rarely issued direct orders and relied on the loyalty and respect of his junior officers to make things happen. As a first lieutenant, I was assigned to a program office responsible for a communications satellite acquisition. A few months into the assignment, we welcomed a new program director with management responsibility for the entire program. He was Colonel Forrest McCartney, and this began the most inspiring, motivational, and educational experience I've had working for anyone.

My introduction to the colonel didn't happen as it usually would. Instead of getting summoned to his office to meet my new commander, he appeared unannounced and sat across from my desk. For the next half hour, we proceeded to talk about everything except work. He wanted to know all about me, and I did most of the talking. By the end of our conversation, he had won me over, and I was sure I would love working for him. I was right. He was a senior officer who could order me to do whatever he wanted, but he got far more out of me by inspiring his team and leading by example.

I quickly discovered that McCartney was a master strategist, consummate salesman, brilliant communicator, top-notch systems engineer, and great leader, all rolled into one. Although smaller than many other defense acquisitions, our satellite program received special attention at the Pentagon because it was managed by the Air Force and funded by the Navy. Some military veterans might consider that arrangement a recipe for disaster. We made quarterly trips to Washington to brief the department secretaries and their staffs about the program status. These Command Assessment Reviews (CAR) could make or break a program, so the pressure was always on to get it exactly right.

In addition to myself, one other company grade officer was responsible for all the financial analysis and reporting for our program. One day, we received a meeting notice from the colonel's office regarding the upcoming CAR. There were no instructions as to what to prepare for the meeting. My partner and I decided to review the last CAR presentation and update it to the extent we could with the latest information. Before the advent of the computer age, we redlined a document by marking up the paper copy with the revisions in red ink. We also talked to the engineers and updated as much of the briefing narrative as possible. We were determined to put a draft package in front of the colonel to facilitate our meeting to the maximum extent possible.

The meeting began with the colonel asking how we were doing and if there was anything he could do for us. He meant it. We said everything was fine, and that we'd assembled a redlined CAR brief-ing for him to review. At that point, our education about executive briefings commenced. He thanked us for our efforts but told us we had done it in reverse sequence from what he wanted. Rather than assemble data that tell a story, he preferred to decide what story we would tell and then figure out what data we needed to back it up. In other words, decide how the story ends and then assemble the pieces that get you to that predetermined outcome. The data wouldn't define or dictate the story; we would.

This approach was a tectonic revelation for a young lieutenant like myself. It directly contradicted most of what I'd learned in school and was the opposite of my normal thought process and logic path. It made perfect sense as I thought about what he said. Never be constrained by numbers or data because you can always make them tell whatever story you want. It's simply a matter of what data you use and how you analyze and display it.

This experience helps explain the "science" behind opinion polling and research. I've always believed that if you tell me what you want a poll to say, I can design one that gives you the desired answer. It's a function of what questions you ask and how they're worded and presented. Change the parameters around, and you'll get a broad assortment of responses. I knew from studying statis-tics that there's a statistic for almost everything, so sorting through them will reveal the ones that support your case, whatever that is.

Instinctively, McCartney knew how to take storytelling to an entirely new level, and I never forgot the lesson learned from that first CAR. I watched him knock it out of the park at the

Pentagon. While these quarterly briefings weren't negotiations in a traditional sense, his ability to persuade such a high-level audience was paramount to the program's success. Earlier, I recommended that you think of negotiating as persuading and influencing people to your way of thinking, regardless of rank or position in the organization. Working for the colonel was the equivalent of a masterclass in accomplishing this without making waves or rocking the boat.

I've often reminded myself of that experience as a refresher course on how to win over doubters and eventually prevail. McCartney constantly reminded us not to get lost in the weeds and to focus on the big picture and the desired endgame. Decide where you want to get to in the grand scheme of things, then figure out the best and most efficient way to get there. I've always kept those objectives in sight during every negotiation I've participated in.

I was promoted to captain within a year of starting this assignment, and McCartney was promoted to brigadier general. Nothing changed. He was who he was, and wearing stars on his shoulders never altered the way he treated his subordinates and superiors. One thing he routinely did always amazed me. Whenever someone outside our organization visited him, regardless of who they were, he would accompany them from his office to their car as they left. Then, on his way back, he'd stop by my office and tell me what they'd agreed to during their walk to the parking lot. This pattern repeated many times with different people even though no agreements coalesced during their initial meetings.

I was fascinated by how successful these walks had become, so I asked him about it one day. He offered two reasons for why he did it. The first was to show respect for his guests and emphasize his appreciation for coming to see him. The second was that he consistently accomplished more goals, finalized more agreements, and cut more deals during the few minutes in the parking lot than he ever did in his office, regardless of how long the meeting was.

I was surprised by the second reason. How was it possible to spend all that time in meetings and reach relatively few conclusions, only to knock out all kinds of deals on the way out the door? There had to be lessons learned that could be applied to successful negotiations. I have some theories on why this strategy worked, but before I outline them, it's worthwhile to share what happened to General McCartney during the latter stages of his career.

His last two military assignments were as commander of the Air Force Space Division and vice commander of the Air Force Space Command, holding the rank of lieutenant general. He was considered one of the top leaders in managing complex space communications and surveillance programs. He was ultimately responsible for successfully executing several complex satellite launch and deployment missions.

After losing the Space Shuttle Challenger in January 1986, subsequent missions were canceled until NASA determined what caused the explosion and corrected it on future flights. In October 1986, McCartney was detailed to NASA as director of its principal launch base to help manage the return-to-flight activities. During this period, he remained on active duty but wore civilian clothes in his new role. Less than a year later, he retired from the Air Force and was selected as the John F. Kennedy Space Center (KSC) director in senior executive service status.

Bringing in an outsider during such a period of turmoil within NASA was met with skepticism by some of the existing staff, but it took only a short time for McCartney to win most (if not all) of them over. He was instrumental in steering the KSC team's efforts to get the Shuttle program back on track.

After a long and distinguished career, McCartney retired to his home near Cape Canaveral in 1992. During the fall of 2012, I planned a business trip to Florida and thought that would be a great time to visit the best boss I've ever had. Hopefully, we could relive old times, but I also had many questions I'd never have asked as his military subordinate. I searched online for his contact info and discovered he had passed away that July after a short illness. It was heartbreaking news, and I was devastated that I hadn't made plans to visit him sooner. We'd lost one of the best of the best.

I intended to ask about all those times he walked his guests to their cars in the parking lot. We'd always discussed the results of those private "meetings" but had never focused on what prompted him to do it in the first place. I always assumed he believed it worked to his advantage, but I wanted to hear his thoughts on that aspect as well. So, without the benefit of the general's insights, all I can offer now are theories that I've incorporated into my thinking on practically every negotiation I've ever done. I've numbered them sequentially to keep track, but they're listed in no particular order.

1. Scheduled meetings foster an air of authority and formality that can suppress and intimidate the participants. That atmosphere isn't conducive to horse-trading and making difficult decisions. McCartney never sat at the head of the conference table in his office. No one ever sat there because he wanted everyone in the room to feel like they shared equally in what transpired and the eventual outcomes. When he was trying to solve a problem, rank didn't matter, whether you were military or civilian.

2. Any sense of formality vanishes and guests naturally let their guard down when the meeting concludes. Once the room empties, it's just McCartney and his senior guest chatting without the pressure of expectations and an audience that can sometimes stifle free thinking and expression. They're more apt to be receptive to ideas and opinions when exposed to a far less controlled environment.

3. If neither party got what they wanted up to that point, they now have a limited window of time available to

achieve a meeting of the minds. This self-imposed pressure forces concessions because neither party wants to go away empty-handed.

4. Once they arrive at the car, it's now or never. Both parties understand that convening another meeting in the future will likely result in more discussions with no resolution. What will be different next time? Are we going to know more then than we do now?

5. Two key people with the requisite power will often make something happen when neither party can foresee a better alternative to what they can get on the spot in real time. Otherwise, nothing is accomplished, and it's back to square one. Time is money, and neither party is in a position to waste it.

I watched this script play out countless times from my office window overlooking the parking lot. Once a meeting broke up, I'd wait a couple of minutes for them to walk to the end of the hallway, down one flight of stairs, and out the door. They'd talk on their way to the car and stand next to the car for a few minutes before shaking hands and going their separate ways. Like clockwork, the general would head straight to my office to provide me with a rundown of what had just happened. I'd write up a description of any agreements and a summary of the discussions. He would sign this document as a memorandum for the record.

I had trouble keeping up with everything I learned by observing the general in action. One lesson that stands out is that you never have to fit any negotiation into an unbreakable mold. Thinking outside the box and developing a unique style give you an advantage that's yours to exploit.

His practice of going one-on-one while walking someone to their car is a tactic I've adopted over the years in various forms. When two negotiating teams have been going at each other for hours, and progress has stalled and bogged down to mutual frustration, it's past the time to take a break. I'll seize that opportunity to pull their team leader aside and suggest a short walk to get our blood flowing again. We might top that off with a snack and a cold drink.

It's in this environment that many substantive negotiations happen. Escape from the noise and focus on the two or three unyielding obstacles blocking the path to cutting a deal. If you're in the ballpark of an agreement at that point, extend the conversation over dinner and an adult beverage or two. Make that time count. It may be your best chance of nailing down an agreement that conquers those immovable barriers.

Closing the Deal

— — — — — — — — — — — — — — — — — —

Patience mitigates and sometimes prevents panic. Lack of patience is one of your worst enemies as a negotiator. The other side will take advantage of that weakness, and you'll rarely get what you want. You must be willing and able to go the distance and play the long game. You can't throw in the towel during the 11th round of a 12-round fight.

We've all succumbed to impatience. You're working on a house project, and you're about 90% complete. You've worked long and hard and can't wait to finish, so you cut a few corners here and there and wrap it up. I've done it. Sometimes, I regretted it and backtracked to finish it the way I should have done it the first time.

Don't make this mistake in a negotiation. Good negotiators will always use your frustration and impatience against you and make you pay. Losing your nerve plays right into their hands, so be patient right up to the finish line. Fight off that temptation to end it regardless of the consequences, and use the endgame to your advantage. You don't have to concede anything. Force the other side to concede.

You can usually tell when you're getting close to a settlement. Both sides have worn through their positions and arguments, and now it comes down to agreeing to what could be an arbitrary number. As I said earlier, I won't propose a split, but I'll entertain such a proposal from the other party. They could be thinking the same thing, which is why all your offers up to that point are so important. Position yourself so that if a split materializes, it will put you at your target number.

Before you get there, exhaust your list of potential trade-offs to narrow the remaining gap. If you want something that can be exchanged for something they want, incorporate a trade at the bottom line. If what they want is worth more than what they offer, you can either ask for more value in trade or offset the differential with money. Be creative, and don't leave anything on the table that could be bartered to get you closer. Scope changes are always an option if both parties can accommodate them into the final agreement.

For those familiar with chess, you're continually evaluating subsequent moves for yourself and your opponent before you make a move. Each move is part of an overall strategy to gain the advantage. Negotiation requires the same type of strategic thinking. Offers should not be singular events concocted in a vacuum. Make one offer to set up the next one and those to follow. Imagine you're cutting a trail, and the idea is to lead the other party down that trail until it ends at the settlement you want.

There are essential elements that will help position you for such a settlement. The first is that the other party has sufficient basis for comparing your position with theirs. For them to make concessions, ensure they understand the basis for your position. That doesn't require you to convince them to agree with it. Even if they do, they'll seldom admit it. Give them sufficient information to blur the bright line between their number and yours. Tilt them in your direction, not topple them, which would increase resistance to your persuasive efforts.

The second element is to ensure the other party's basic needs and priorities are satisfied, so long as doing so doesn't weaken your overall position. This is especially true if you're buying something in a private sale. People form emotional attachments to their possessions that don't translate into higher market value from the buyer's perspective. If I'm buying the first car you owned that has collector value, there's an excellent chance you're reluctant to part with it. In addition to making you a fair offer, I want you to feel comfortable with me as the new owner. That includes assurances that I'll maintain and care for the car like you've done over the years. The burden is on the buyer to establish a comfort level with the seller that convinces him you're the number one choice to assume responsibility for his treasure.

Several years ago, I was in the market for a used car through a private sale. I located one in excellent condition with low mileage. The asking price was below what I believed was fair market value, so I was sure there would be many other potential buyers. I knew this wouldn't be a price negotiation and that I might have to offer more than the asking price to increase my leverage. Offering more goes against all my instincts, but sometimes you do what you have to do.

I called to accept his offer at the asking price, conditioned only on my vehicle inspection and that I would pay in cash. He didn't answer the phone, so I left a message with those stipulations, but I didn't stop there. I briefly explained why I wanted his car and that I hoped he would seriously consider my offer. I was very polite and succinct and did my best to convey I was reliable and would conclude the sale if we agreed on the terms. My goal was to allay any fears that I would back out of the deal and put him in a tough position. If he informed potential buyers that the car was sold, they might drop out of the picture and not return.

He called me back later that evening and said he'd received over two dozen calls since his ad went public several hours earlier. He was returning my call based on the message I'd left and that he wanted me to own the car. I went to look at it the next day and took it for a test drive. I liked it, and he drove me to the Department of Motor Vehicles to transfer the title in real time. I thanked him for everything and asked how he had decided to sell me the car when he had many other options. He told me about some of the calls he'd received and how they had all left him completely unimpressed. He was selling the car for his daughter, who didn't have time to manage the sale, and they wanted to avoid any stumbling blocks that would prevent it from getting done quickly and efficiently. My unvarnished, straightforward message had given him that confidence.

I relate this story to illustrate that negotiating is the art of persuasion and that being aggressive or challenging is often the wrong approach. I knew it wouldn't work here because I understood the supply and demand situation, which virtually eliminated my leverage. When you find yourself in that position, you adapt and find a way to create leverage out of nowhere. My best chance to accomplish that was to present myself as an authentic, willing, and able buyer who would follow through to complete the deal. It worked.

An integral part of the formula of getting what you want depends on determining what you believe to be an acceptable outcome for the other party. The negotiation isn't all about you and your needs, and if the other party won't play ball, the game's over. What constitutes an acceptable outcome for the other party may be a combination of different things that aren't necessarily tied solely to price. While price is a high priority, it may not be the top priority.

Understanding the other side's imperatives is just as important as understanding your own, so figure out what you would do if you were in their shoes. When constructing offers, attempt to satisfy some of their priorities if doing so doesn't weaken your overall position beyond what you're willing to accept. Be prepared to give up the little things to shield and protect the big things you won't concede. Know your limits and how far you'll go on all aspects of the deal.

A person's needs in a negotiation don't always equate solely to money. My father owned a terrific vinyl record collection that contained the great bandleaders from the big band era. When he worked in the radio business, he interviewed several of them and had presale access to their records as they were released.

When he decided to sell his collection, he asked me to find a buyer who would appreciate the music as much as he did and wasn't looking to flip it for profit on a resale. It happened exactly that way. The buyer never discussed the price with me or my father. He was far more interested in how my father assembled the collection and his connections with bandleaders like Goodman, Ellington, Shaw, Basie, and Miller.

My father's willingness and enthusiasm to tell him several stories about the swing era and give him inside information about the arrangers and musicians persuaded the buyer to pay the asking price. Money wasn't even a factor. The buyer's needs were satisfied, and my father was confident we'd found someone who would cherish the collection as much as he had.

The third element is that the other party believes they played a credible role in achieving the outcome and is fully invested in the result. This is critical, even though it may not accurately reflect your record of the events leading to the settlement. Perception often eclipses reality when it comes to negotiation, so the burden is on you to construct an endgame that has them believing what you want them to believe. One way to achieve this is to recount the details in a summary fashion that illuminates your attention to and consideration for their position. Review a few of the nuggets they offered during discussions that directly influenced the direction and slope of the bottom-line number.

One thing to be conscious of throughout a negotiation is the concession rate. To illustrate the point, assume a seller offers you a used car for $10,000. Your first counteroffer is $6,000. If the seller drops his price by $1,000 to $9,000, should your counteroffer reflect an equal move up by $1,000 to $7,000? That might be their expectation, but what you do should depend on your price objective. If you offer $7,000 and copy their concession rate of $1,000, you're signaling that you're willing to settle at $8,000, halfway between the respective starting positions. If that's not your objective, don't send that signal.

Whether you like it or not, or whether it's fair or not, there may be an expectation by the other party that your concession rate will at least equal theirs. It's equivalent to splitting the difference between the original positions. Never fall into this trap. You don't want to make offers that give the slightest indication that you're angling for an eventual split, with the possible exception of the concluding offers at the final stage of a negotiation.

This trap is easy to avoid by not doing it. Sometimes, I'll concede more than the other party in one move to create the impression that a split is the last thing on my mind. I'll follow that up on the next move by offering significantly less than they did on their prior move. Without being predictable, you make successive offers that don't follow a straight line to your endgame. This technique keeps them guessing and off guard, which is precisely where you want them.

Structure your offers to influence a concession rate for the other party that signals they want closure. If you don't attain the expected concession rate, alter your strategy as you go along. You can't make big moves if theirs are tiny, especially if your starting point left you little margin to play with. This is why the first offer or counteroffer is so critical. It becomes your baseline against which all subsequent offers will be compared and measured. At the beginning, leave yourself plenty of margin to trade away later. I can't overemphasize how important this is.

As you close in on a handshake, keep in mind that people have an aversion to losses that exceed the potential for gains. An example is how they invest in stocks during a bear market. Rather than sell stocks as they start to decline, they'll hold them, hoping prices will eventually revert to where they were. The better play is to take profits on those stocks and short stocks to make money on the way down. Most people won't do that because they fear the market will turn around and put them in a loss position. They'll assume more risk to avoid paper losses than to realize actual gains. Place yourself in a stronger position by understanding this mentality when the risk of loss is an issue in arriving at a settlement.

Never conclude a negotiation without a "meeting of the minds" that includes a written narrative of what both parties agreed to and that both parties signed and dated. At a minimum, the basis of the bargain should consist of the following elements wherever applicable: price (in proper denomination), statement of work (scope), identification and quantities of goods or services, delivery schedule, performance incentives (if any), express warranties (if any), terms and conditions, and any documents incorporated by reference. People tend to forget what just happened, either intentionally or unintentionally. Complete documentation will help avert a court battle to prove the elements of an agreement.

Successful negotiation requires a sense of timing, creativity, keen awareness, and the ability to anticipate the other party's next move. Depending on the respective concession rates, your moves should get progressively smaller, and you can expect the same from the other party.

Resist the temptation to split the remaining difference as a central part of your endgame. If for no other reason, don't do it strictly on principle, particularly if you'll engage in recurring negotiations with the same people. It's a bad precedent and indicates you're agreeable to arbitrary moves with no rational basis. Do your best to avoid it.

Final Thoughts

‾‾ ‾‾ ‾‾ ‾‾ ‾‾ ‾‾ ‾‾ ‾‾ ‾‾ ‾‾ ‾‾ ‾‾ ‾‾ ‾‾ ‾‾

This book is jam-packed with my opinions. That's all they are—opinions. By now, you should have a fairly good idea of how I think and connect the dots. What you just finished reading represents what has worked for me over several decades negotiating billions of dollars' worth of contracts. You read, "The one thing that differentiates every negotiation I've done is the people on the other side of the table." Once you get past that, you'll find that most negotiations follow a relatively predictable path. There will always be exceptions, but that's more due to the people involved rather than the subject matter at hand.

You read, "Negotiation is an art, not a science, so there are no right or wrong answers." Unlike science, no universal rules or practices exist regarding a specific negotiation. Your challenge is to pick and choose the tactics and strategies you believe will work on that day in that negotiation. Adaptability is crucial because if you lock yourself into a losing strategy, it will be tough to backpedal your way out. You need to be quick of mind and fast on your feet to stay on the track that will propel you to your goal.

If you're uncertain about your next move, always revert to the basic principles guided by common sense. Don't make it more complicated than it already is. Stay positive and keep your emotions at bay. Remain focused, think clearly, and keep your eye on the big picture. Don't allow yourself to be sidetracked by extraneous chatter and inconsequential barriers that may frustrate you as you implement your strategy. Overcome those barriers by reminding the other party that your shared mission of reaching an agreement is unachievable if a roadblock appears at every turn. Shatter those barriers to make genuine progress and enlist their help in making that happen.

Never let the other side knock you off your game. Like a major league baseball pitcher, top negotiators have an arsenal of pitches to throw at you, and you'll never know for sure what's coming next: curveball, slider, cutter, fastball, splitter, screwball, changeup, sinker, knuckleball, sweeper, slurve, or forkball. A batter must anticipate the type of pitch with very few clues to rely on. Most of it is a function of raw talent, training, instinct, and experience. Even when they guess correctly, they must still judge the swing and make solid contact with the ball. They also learn from their mistakes. Rather than be defeated by a strikeout, professionals come back in the next inning determined not to repeat those mistakes.

I'll be the first to admit that negotiating is infinitely easier than hitting a 100 MPH fastball. You have to be ready for the unexpected and not let the other side think for one second that you've been caught off guard. I can't overstate the importance of the psychological advantage gained by exuding confidence and intelligence. It's an effective way to intimidate the other side and convince them you're not in this to compromise but to win.

The so-called experts would have you believe that the best-case scenario is a win-win negotiation where both parties walk away thinking they got most of what they wanted. To be blunt, I'm not an ardent fan of win-win negotiations, nor do I routinely subscribe to conventional wisdom. I subscribe to win-lose negotiations where I win while still convincing the other side that they won. I'm not looking for fairness or equitable outcomes where both sides reap comparable benefits. I expect to come away with far more than they did. If I don't, then in my mind, I've lost. I'm there for one reason and one reason only: To win, period.

If you disagree with any of my points and recommendations, I respect your opinion. Hopefully, you have a sound basis for your opinion that will explain why you believe I've missed the mark. I'm always wide open to great ideas and critical thinking. I've absorbed tremendous feedback during my seminars and learned by listening to attendees' constructive comments. Some of it has made its way into this book in one form or another, resulting in a better source of information based on proven experiences beyond my own.

Walk into every negotiation and do what works for you. I've dealt with great negotiators over the years who were distinctive in many ways. However, the common thread weaving through their negotiation approaches is that they all followed the fundamental principles outlined in this book. The differences I noted were primarily in the methods and techniques they used to apply those principles. You might call it a difference in style rather than substance.

We don't often choose the people we negotiate with, particularly in a business setting where the other company dictates who represents them. I've sparred with people with diverse backgrounds, educations, personalities, styles, methods, and a few unusual and entertaining quirks for good measure. You must adapt and think on the fly to successfully navigate whatever they throw at you. My go-to mindset is to revert to the fundamental principles and start from there. I wouldn't call them fundamental principles if I didn't believe they have foundational qualities that I encourage every negotiator to embrace.

Sensing I was approaching my closing kick and sprint to the tape, I made a list of random thoughts, some that you haven't seen and others that may be variations of what you've already read. I include them here in short form because they're important concepts that popped into my head as I neared the finish line.

- **Businesses that can't negotiate effectively will be significantly disadvantaged in the competitive marketplace. Their success ultimately depends on it.**

- Just because you're not negotiating doesn't mean the other party isn't.

- Understanding people and their businesses is usually more important than being an expert on a specific product you're interested in purchasing from them.

- Take notes and spit back the facts because the cheapest concession you can make is to assure the other party they've been heard.

- Make your first offer bold, aggressive, and designed to spark a palpable reaction from the other side. Spike the needle on their barometer. Remind yourself of a quote attributed to World War II bomber pilots: "If you're not catching flak, you're not over the target."

- Always set a reasonable date and time when every offer and counteroffer will expire.

- Keep listening. Emulate Silent Cal. "Your problem, governor, is that you talk back."

- I've never had anyone invite me to negotiate with them or tell me they were willing to negotiate. Why would they? You can always begin negotiations by making the first offer. If they won't negotiate, you've lost absolutely nothing. Never be afraid to make the first move.

- Leverage is power. In fact, leverage is everything. Unless you have at least 51% of the leverage, it's going to be much tougher to get what you want. Find it. Create it. Use leverage forcefully by focusing on your strengths and the other party's weaknesses.

- Speaking of leverage, it's too bad you're not a baby. Start bawling, and you get anything you want, whenever you want it. That may represent the ultimate example of instantaneous, irrefragable leverage that's absolutely priceless.

- Something is worth what someone else is willing and able to pay for it. No more and no less. Remember that.

- "A picture paints a thousand words." Hard facts and data that support your position are incredibly compelling in graphic form. A graph of the national debt going hyperbolic is far more impactful than the raw numbers. Hardly anyone will remember the numbers, but they'll remember that ugly graph.

- Put yourself in the other party's shoes and find a way to satisfy their basic needs. What does an acceptable outcome look like for them?

- My take: The average negotiation is 30% experience, 20% psychology and intuition, 20% judgment and common sense, 10% strategy, 10% preparation, and 10% timing. It doesn't always work out that way, but it's in the ballpark. If you have minimal experience, preparation and strategy take on a much more prominent role.

- Establishing a psychological advantage has been an essential ingredient of my most successful negotiations. I use it to offset leverage shortfalls and other weaknesses in my position. It's a form of mind over matter.

- I've negotiated with dozens of people whom I didn't know and who had never earned my trust. We don't always get to choose who we negotiate with. Trust in either direction is not necessarily needed to negotiate if you stick to the fundamental principles.

- Confidence and self-assuredness will gain you the respect of worthy adversaries. I never cross the line and fall into rudeness and obnoxiousness. Elevate yourself into the position of being able to dictate the mood, tempo, and direction of the negotiation.

- I'd much rather win an agreement than an argument.

- Avoid surprises by anticipating them before they happen. Like in chess, always be thinking well beyond your next move.

- Where you finish a negotiation is heavily dependent on where you start it. While this may seem intuitively obvious, you'd be amazed at how many people fail to realize how foundational this tenet is until it's too late.

- Never offer to split the difference to settle a negotiation. If the other party proposes a split, you can accept or reject it, or position yourself to set up a double-split.

- Don't assume your lawyer has the skills to negotiate effectively. If he does, great. If he doesn't, you know what to do.

- You're on a mission: Get what you want at the price you want. The tools you need to accomplish it are here for the taking.

I struggled to come up with a way to wrap this up. Thinking back on the negotiations I've done, after doing everything I could to get what I wanted, I reached a brick wall that blocked my last push to the finish line. Long-distance runners refer to this as "bonking" or "hitting the wall." During the latter stages of a race, they can experience sudden fatigue and a rapid drop-off in energy. When these symptoms are elevated to extreme levels, the brain may shut down the body's systems to save itself. Elite runners know how to safely break through the wall and win races.

While negotiating presents none of those personal risks, top negotiators find a way to crack that wall just enough to close the deal without causing it to collapse. It's not easy to do consistently. I'd compare it to the feeling I've had when tightening a screw into a piece of wood, and I'm almost done. I sense that one more turn of the screwdriver will strip the head of the screw, making it extremely difficult to keep tightening or remove it and start over. In a negotiation, this is the point where it seems like the other party won't bend any more than they already have, and my gut is telling me to end it right there. Otherwise, if I push any harder, the whole deal might fall apart in a matter of seconds.

This is when I'm going to break you. When you feel like you've hit the wall in a negotiation, you find a way to take that last step that achieves your goal. You don't hesitate. You don't back down. You don't regroup. You don't rethink your strategy. You hit that wall with a final blow, crack it open, and take your victory lap.

Thank you very much for reading my book. Life is short, and your time is precious, so I'm humbled that you chose to spend some of it with me. Even if you don't agree with everything I've written, I'm confident you'll think about some of the tactics and strategies I've suggested the next time you find yourself embroiled in a tough negotiation. Getting you to think about what you're doing and about to do is a solid victory on my scorecard. While I can't guarantee what works for me will work for you in the same way, I know I've given you food for thought. What you do with it is totally your call.

At the very least, I hope you picked up a few valuable nuggets to help you in your future negotiations. I bet you save more than enough money in your next negotiation to pay for this book. You're already way ahead if you didn't have to buy it.

I'll leave you with one of my favorite quotes from President John F. Kennedy's inaugural address on 20 January 1961: "Let us never negotiate out of fear, but let us never fear to negotiate."

Take care and good luck!

Geoff Michael

www.ingramcontent.com/pod-product-compliance
Lightning Source LLC
Chambersburg PA
CBHW020231130626
46549CB00005B/1833